ENDURING, SURVIVING, AND THRIVING AS A LAW ENFORCEMENT EXECUTIVE

The Illinois Law Enforcement
Training and Standards Board
Springfield, Illinois

ENDURING, SURVIVING, AND THRIVING AS A LAW ENFORCEMENT EXECUTIVE

Edited by

THOMAS J. JURKANIN, PH.D.
LARRY T. HOOVER, PH.D.
JERRY L. DOWLING, J.D.
JANICE AHMAD

Charles C Thomas
PUBLISHER • LTD.
SPRINGFIELD • ILLINOIS • U.S.A.

Published and Distributed Throughout the World by

CHARLES C THOMAS • PUBLISHER, LTD.
2600 South First Street
Springfield, Illinois 62704

This book is protected by copyright. No part of
it may be reproduced in any manner without
written permission from the publisher.

© 2001 by CHARLES C THOMAS • PUBLISHER, LTD.

ISBN 0-398-07116-0 (hard)
ISBN 0-398-07117-9 (paper)

Library of Congress Catalog Card Number: 00-057737

With THOMAS BOOKS *careful attention is given to all details of manufacturing and design. It is the Publisher's desire to present books that are satisfactory as to their physical qualities and artistic possibilities and appropriate for their particular use.* THOMAS BOOKS *will be true to those laws of quality that assure a good name and good will.*

Printed in the United States of America
RR-R-3

Library of Congress Cataloging-in-Publication Data

Enduring, surviving, and thriving as a law enforcement executive/edited by Thomas J. Jurkanin, Larry T. Hoover, Jerry L. Dowling, Janice Ahmad.
   p. cm.
   At head of title: Illinois Law Enforcement Training and Standards Board, Springfield, Illinois.
   Includes bibliographical references and index.
   ISBN 0-398-07116-0 – ISBN 0-398-07117-9
   1. Police administration. I. Jurkanin, Thomas J., II. Hoover, Larry T. III. Dowling, Jerry L. IV. Ahmad, Janice.
   IV. Illinois Law Enforcement Training and Standards Board.

HV7935 b.E53 2000
363.2'068–dc21

00-057737

CONTRIBUTORS

JANICE AHMAD

Janice Ahmad is a doctoral candidate in the College of Criminal Justice at Sam Houston State University. In addition to researching and writing her dissertation, she is currently the research project manager of a National Institute of Justice, Office of Science and Technology, grant. Prior to this, Ms. Ahmad was a project manager at Justex Systems, Inc., as well as a police officer and director of a prosecutor-based victim/witness assistance program.

DR. LEWIS G. BENDER

Dr. Bender is a Professor of Public Administration at Southern Illinois University at Edwardsville. He teaches courses in supervision, leadership and policy analysis. He received his Ph.D. from the University of Georgia and consults in the areas of organizational planning and development.

DONALD L. CUNDIFF

Chief Cundiff started his law enforcement career in West Covina, California in 1961. He has served as Chief of Police in Woodstock, Rolling Meadows and Hoffman Estates, Illinois. He retired in 1997 with 36 years of law enforcement experience, 20 years serving as chief of police. Chief Cundiff holds a Masters Degree from Western Illinois University.

BENNETT W. DICKMANN

Bennett W. Dickmann served as Director of Police (Chief) in Edwardsville, Illinois for 25 years. He currently serves as the

City Administrator. Chief Dickmann holds a Bachelor of Science Degree in Business Administration from Southern Illinois University.

CARL DOBBS

Chief Dobbs served 28 years with the Wheaton, Illinois Police Department, retiring in 1996. He subsequently served as Interim Police Chief in Northlake and in Bensenville, Illinois. Chief Dobbs was a member of the criminal justice faculty at the College of DuPage and is a past president of the Illinois Association of Chiefs of Police. He holds a Bachelors Degree from Aurora University.

DONALD DONESKE

Donald Doneske retired after serving over 40 years as a law enforcement officer and executive. Doneske was appointed Chief of Police of the Riverside, Illinois Police Department in 1973 and served in that capacity until his recent retirement. Chief Doneske served as a Governor appointee to the Illinois Law Enforcement Training and Standards Board and served a two year term as Chairman of the Board.

DR. JERRY L. DOWLING

Jerry L. Dowling earned his Doctor of Jurisprudence degree from The University of Tennessee and has been a professor at the College of Criminal Justice, Sam Houston State University (SHSU) since 1972. His primary areas of teaching and research include criminal law, pretrial criminal procedure, and the legal aspects of criminal justice management. In addition to his academic duties, Professor Dowling has conducted numerous law enforcement training seminars on legal issues affecting police officers and police administrators. He currently teaches as a faculty member at the Bill Blackwood Law Enforcement Management Institute. Prior to joining the faculty of SHSU, Dowling worked as a Special Agent with the Federal Bureau of Investigation. He has authored several publications in the field of criminal procedure and police personnel practices. He is a principal in Justex Systems, Inc., a public safety labor relations consulting firm, and serves as Editor of *Police Labor Monthly* and *Fire Service Labor Monthly* newsletters.

DR. ROBERT J. FISCHER

Dr. Robert J. Fischer received his Ph.D. from Southern Illinois University and has been on the Law Enforcement Justice Administration (LEJA) faculty at Western Illinois University since 1975. Dr. Fischer, the past Chairperson of the LEJA department, is the Director of the Illinois Law Enforcement Training and Standards Board's Executive Institute. He is the Senior Editor of the *Journal of Security Administration* and Editor of the new *Illinois Law Enforcement Executive Forum*. Dr. Fischer is widely published with articles in *Police Chief, Security Management,* and other journals. He is also the author of several texts.

GEORGE P. GRAVES

George P. Graves began his law enforcement career in Western Springs, Illinois in 1958. In 1965, he was appointed chief and later assumed the position of Chief of Police with the Village of Downers Grove. He recently retired with 40 years in law enforcement and 35 years as chief. Chief Graves served as Secretary-Treasurer of the Illinois FBINAA Chapter, President of the Illinois Association of Chiefs of Police and as a founder of the Suburban Law Enforcement Academy at the College of DuPage.

SAMUEL D. HILLER

Samuel D. Hiller began his law enforcement career in 1958 with the Illinois State Police. He retired from the State Police in 1986 at the rank of master sergeant to assume the Office of Sheriff of Perry County, Illinois. Hiller held the Office of Sheriff for three terms, 12 years, and retired in 1998. Sheriff

Hiller is a graduate of Southern Illinois University with a Bachelor of Science Degree in Police Administration.

DR. LARRY HOOVER

Dr. Larry Hoover, received his Ph.D. from Michigan State University and has been on the criminal justice faculty at Sam Houston State University (SHSU) since 1977. Dr. Hoover, a past president of the Academy of Criminal Justice Sciences, is director of the Police Research Center at SHSU. He is also a principal of Justex Systems, Inc. A former police officer in Lansing, Michigan and training coordinator with the Michigan Law Enforcement Officers Training Council, he also served on the faculty at Michigan State University. His endeavors include editing the Texas Law Enforcement Management and Administrative Statistics monthly bulletin series, teaching in the Bill Blackwood Law Enforcement Management Institute, conducting research for SHSU's Community Policing Institute, directing a technology transfer grant from the National Institute of Justice, and directing a major information system development project, CRIMES, for SHSU. He is editor of the anthologies *Police Management: Issues and Perspectives, Quantifying Quality in Policing,* and *Police Program Evaluation,* all published by the Police Executive Research Forum.

DR. THOMAS J. JURKANIN

Dr. Jurkanin serves as the Executive Director of the Illinois Law Enforcement Training and Standards Board, a position he has held since 1992. He has 25 years of experience in the policing field. Dr. Jurkanin holds a Ph.D. from Southern Illinois University in Education and Social Justice. Dr. Jurkanin serves as Vice Chairman of the Governors Law Enforcement Medal of Honor Committee.

GEORGE F. KOERTGE

George F. Koertge has served as Executive Director of the

Illinois Association of Chiefs of Police since 1990. A former police chief, Koertge is a Certified Association Executive (CAE) and chairs the Executive Directors Section of the State Association of Chiefs of Police (SACOP), a division of the International Association of Chiefs of Police. Koertge received his Bachelors Degree from Lewis University.

CHARLES R. MCDONALD

Charles R. McDonald recently retired as Chief of Police of the Southern Illinois University at Edwardsville. He had served in a similar capacity at Central Connecticut State University, New Britain, Connecticut. McDonald has over 23 years of experience as a police administrator. Chief McDonald is past president of the Illinois Association of Chiefs of Police, and served as a member of the Illinois Law Enforcement Training and Standards Board for the past eight years. Currently Chief McDonald is a Police Training Specialist employed by the Board. McDonald holds a Bachelors Degree in Business Administration from Central Connecticut State University.

JOHN J. MILLNER

John J. Millner has been employed by the Elmhurst, Illinois Police Department since 1972. He was appointed Chief of Police in 1986. He currently serves as First Vice President of the Illinois Association of Chiefs of Police and serves on many criminal justice committees and commissions by appointment of the Governor and the Attorney General. Chief Millner has extensive experience as an instructor in the areas of police communication, interviewing and interrogations and the politics of policing. He holds a Master of Arts Degree from Western Illinois University in law enforcement administration.

ROBERT J. NOONAN

Robert J. Noonan began his law enforcement career in 1968. He served as Chief of Police in Troy, Illinois for eights years, and currently is Chief of Police of the Wentzville, Missouri Police Department. He has instructed at Columbia College and at the St. Charles County, Missouri Police Academy. Chief Noonan holds a dual Masters Degree in Management and Human Resource Development from Webster University.

RONALD W. PAVLOCK

Ronald W. Pavlock has served as a chief in Illinois since 1977. He currently serves as Chief of Police in Mount Prospect, Illinois, a position he has held for 19 years. He is past president of the Illinois Association of Chiefs of Police. Chief Pavlock holds a Bachelor of Arts Degree, Summa Cum Laude, from the University of Minnesota and a Masters of Public Administration from Syracuse University, New York.

WILLIAM W. PIERCE

William W. Pierce joined the Illinois State Police in 1957 and rose through the ranks to Deputy Superintendent/Field Operations Command in 1979. He received numerous awards and commendations including the Governors Award for Valor and recognition in the prestigious Parade Magazine—*I.A.C.P.* and the Law Enforcement Award for Distinguished and Dedicated Service. Upon retiring from the Illinois State Police in 1985, he was appointed as the Director of Public Safety/Chief of Police in Highland, Illinois until his recent retirement with over 41 years of law enforcement service.

RICHARD A. RANDALL

Richard A. Randall was elected Sheriff in Kendall County, Illinois in 1986 and is currently serving his fourth, four-year term. He previously served as Chief of Police in Yorkville, Illinois and has been involved in law enforcement and community service since 1968. Sheriff Randall is a graduate of Waubonsee Community College, and the FBI National Academy.

ROGER A. RICHARDS

Roger A. Richards began his law enforcement career in 1971 and served as Chief of Police of the Fairview Heights, Illinois Police Department for 21 years. He is past president of the Illinois Association of Chiefs of Police. Currently, Richards serves as Director of the Southwestern Illinois Law Enforcement Commission Mobile Team Training Unit. He is a graduate of the FBI National Academy and holds a Bachelor of Arts Degree.

JAMES L. ROCHE

James L. Roche served as Chief of Police for the cities of St. Charles, Illinois and Crete, Nebraska. He also was Deputy Chief of Police for the Village of Wheeling, Illinois. Roche is past president of the Illinois Association of Chiefs of Police and retired as a Lieutenant Colonel from the Illinois Army National Guard. He currently serves as a Federal Coordination Officer with the Federal Emergency Management Agency. Roche holds a Masters Degree in Public Administration from the University of Nebraska at Omaha.

GARY J. SCHIRA

Gary J. Schira has served as Chief of Police of the Bloomingdale, Illinois Police Department for the past 16 years. Chief Schira is past president of the Illinois Association of Chiefs of Police and is currently a Governor appointee to the Illinois Law Enforcement Training and Standards Board. He is a graduate of the FBI National Academy, PERF's Senior Management Institute affiliated with the Kennedy School of Government and Harvard University. He holds a Masters Degree in Public Administration from Northern Illinois University.

JOHN H. SCHLAF

Chief John H. Schlaf has served as a police officer with the Galesburg, Illinois Police Department since 1967 and was appointed Chief of Police in 1989. He serves as a Governor appointee to the Illinois Law Enforcement Training and Standards Board. Chief Schlaf is a graduate of the FBI National Academy and holds a Bachelors Degree in Criminal Justice from Western Illinois University. He is a veteran of the United States Air Force.

PATRICK F. VAUGHAN

Patrick F. Vaughan currently serves as Deputy Director of the Illinois Law Enforcement Training and Standards Board. His law enforcement career spans 38 years. Vaughan retired from the Decatur, Illinois Police Department as Chief of Police. Later, Vaughan served as Law Enforcement Manager for the U. S. Attorney, Central District of Illinois and presented for the U. S. Department of Justice training programs. He is a graduate of the FBI National Academy and holds a Bachelor's Degree, with graduate study.

FOREWORD

LAW ENFORCEMENT AGENCIES NATIONWIDE are facing increased public and political scrutiny as they operate in a milieu of complex cultural, organizational and societal change. Never before has the citizenry and its institutions, e.g., government, media, community groups, legal systems, demanded so much of law enforcement officials, while concurrently critiquing their actions. Police organizations are under review.

Police agencies must strike a balance between retaining and refining organizational elements that have proven operationally effective, and taking the risks necessary for continuous innovation, renewal and organizational rebirth. Stated in other terms, police agencies must remain traditional, when traditional methods have proven effective, but must be willing to abandon traditionalism when the old way of doing things is no longer effective. As Margaret Meade once stated, "The world in which we are born is not the world in which we will live, nor is it the world in which we will die. " Police managers of today and of tomorrow face an interesting dilemma. What do we keep; what do we throw away; what has worked; what has proven ineffectual and what do we modify? Do we change for sake of change by following every new and emerging professional fad, or do we cautiously resist and risk being labeled as out of touch and out of date?

It is the leadership of law enforcement agencies which has the most significant and immediate effect upon the delivery of constitutional, civil, enlightened, and effective law enforcement. Simply stated, if we strive for effective police organizations and service delivery, we must first develop effective police administrators. This book is designed to assist current and future police executives in sorting through important leadership and management issues.

The genesis of this book was a law enforcement executive retreat conducted in the state of Illinois. The Law Enforcement Training and Standards Board was interested in identifying skills, abilities, knowledge, and personal attributes important to surviving as a law enforcement executive. Contemporary literature abounds with documentation on the limited tenure of police executives. However, Board staff knew of several chiefs and sheriffs who had served the same community consecutively for 20 or more years. This awareness led to the following line of inquiry, "What factors had contributed to their survival?" Do these chiefs and sheriffs hold knowledge and professional secrets that could be shared with others preparing for leadership positions? And importantly, is it possible to survive as a police chief or sheriff without also being viewed as effective?

Invitations to the executive retreat were sent to 20 law enforcement executives, who were deemed to be well respected throughout the state by their peers and by their respective communities, and who had served as police executives for 20 or more years. The executive retreat was conducted in a resort atmosphere, was scheduled to last two days, and had no formalized agenda or scheduled guest speakers. The objective of the retreat was to ask one question of the participant chief executives, "What has made you successful as a law enforcement executive?" In popular vernacular, these law enforcement executives had been there, done that. Our question was, How did you do that?

What started out with looks of doubt from the invited participants and the unstated question of, "What! You called me here for this?" slowly developed into reflection and to a realization of the importance of the question.

It was obvious that many of these old hands had not really given serious consideration to the myriad factors contributing to their extended successes. They had learned and adapted throughout their careers; they had made mistakes and overcome obstacles; they made positive incremental adjustments; and, they had endured, survived, and thrived.

In this experiment the Law Enforcement Training and Standards Board had a selfish, yet laudable, interest in answering the question of "What made you successful as a law enforcement executive?" If the Board is to effectively train new law enforcement leaders, a body of knowledge concerning the state of the practice must be identified. Philosophy and theory combined with day-to-day application and practice was the body of knowledge we sought to identify. Our hypothesis was that 20 years of experience multiplied by 20 participants would yield 400 years of applied application and practice as law enforcement executives.

What began as a two-day executive retreat, focused on one question, developed into a series of three more executive retreats, the development of a week-long course curriculum for newly–appointed law enforcement administrators (see the appendix) and the publishing of this book.

Many of the original contributors to this work currently serve as instructors in the law enforcement administrators course—law enforcement executives with considerable experience, teaching our law enforcement leaders of tomorrow. As experienced law enforcement leaders, they feel an important obligation to give back to the profession and to assist in the development of future law enforcement leaders.

The insights, perspectives, suggestions, warnings, concepts and ideas contained within this book codify years of wisdom and experience related to law enforcement leadership and management. Returning to our earlier proposition, what do we keep, what do we throw away, and what do we modify?–that is the challenge to law enforcement leaders of tomorrow. But, it was also the challenge of law enforcement leaders who began their careers 20 years ago. It is the wise person indeed who learns from the lesson of the past in order to prepare for the future; who holds a healthy appreciation for tradition, but is open to challenge, exploration, inquiry, and change.

Thomas J. Jurkanin, Ph.D.

PREFACE

A PERENNIAL CONCERN VOICED BY POLICE CHIEFS AND SHERIFFS from large and small departments is: you can do it correctly, you can be professional and still lose your job. The recent dismissals of chiefs over political differences with mayors or city councils are indicative of the job tenure problems faced by many law enforcement executives. Today, police chiefs are less secure in their positions than ever before. A scandal is no longer a necessary requisite to dismissal. The days of the police chiefs position as one of the most secure in local government have given way to a decade in which the position may be one of the least secure (Mahtesian, 1997).

Currently, the Police Executive Research Forum estimates that the average large city police chief will last anywhere from two-and-a-half to four years on the job. However, as Charles Mahtesian noted in a recent article in *Governing* magazine: "The sacking of the police chief has become part of the routine of the 1990s" (p.19). The issue of long-term survival has become the hot topic among law enforcement executives. Organizations such as the Police Executive Research Forum have initiated studies that attempt to measure and track the length of tenure among executives in the profession.

There is considerable debate as to why the rate of turnover among chiefs is increasing. As with any job, there are circumstances the officeholder can control or at least influence, while other environmental factors are beyond the control of the individual. Factors likely contributing to increased turnover include: (1) increases in the number of competing constituencies chiefs must appease, (2) new demands and expectations of police departments and police chiefs, and (3) the perception that all government (including police programs) are part of the problem, not the solution, in our society. One cannot measure the impact of any one of these factors on local law enforcement executive turnover. However, it is reasonable to suggest that they collectively have influenced police executive tenure.

These and many other social, political and organizational forces can impact upon the failure or success of a law enforcement executive's career. The purpose of this book is to provide a guide to future and present police chiefs, sheriffs and other law enforcement executives on how to survive and ultimately thrive in a job that is becoming increasingly difficult to handle.

The content taps the collective wisdom of a group of Illinois police chiefs, sheriffs and law enforcement executives with significant tenure in their roles. The contributing law enforcement officials represent large and small departments; urban, suburban and rural areas; and middle, lower and upper income communities. The information, ideas, and suggestions throughout the book were developed in a series of executive forums during which successful law enforcement executives discussed the factors that positively and negatively impacted on their careers. As a guide, this book reflects the perspectives of individuals who have successfully weathered the challenges of law enforcement leadership. While it is not possible to provide advice or a guide that anticipates all circumstances or is universally applicable, this volume provides reference points instructive to professionals facing the demands of law enforcement leadership.

The observations of the participants in the executive forums were compiled in draft documents. The coordinating authors, Larry Hoover, Jerry Dowling, and Janice Ahmad, organized these into chapters; added material from their personal experiences in working with police executives from throughout the country; and integrated published references.

This book examines the question of law enforcement executive survival from three perspectives: demands upon the individual, demands from within the police department, and external/environmental pressures. The information presented provides guidance from the collective experience of the contributors. Through experiences and learning moments as police chiefs, the contributors want to pass on their insight regarding the responsibilities and challenges police chiefs face. On the way up the career ladder most chiefs attend a number of good programs such as the FBI Academy, Law Enforcement Executive Development School (LEEDS), Northwestern Traffic Institute Staff and Command and Police Supervisors School, and the Southern Police Institute. Coupled with formal education, these programs provide a sound backdrop for executing responsibilities. However, the actual application of skills and knowledge is where more learning takes place.

While the contributors cannot provide all the answers to being an effective police chief, an attempt is made to help the reader with her/his new responsibilities. The reader may use this collaborative compilation of information as a guide to prepare for the challenge of being a police chief.

Larry T. Hoover

ACKNOWLEDGMENTS

First and foremost, the Illinois Law Enforcement Training and Standards Board would like to thank each law enforcement executive identified herein who graciously shared their time, experiences and knowledge. Their collective wisdom is documented within this book. Since the nucleus of the book is the contribution of Illinois law enforcement, royalties from its sale are being donated to the Law Enforcement Foundation of Illinois, a non-profit organization supporting activities such as Police and Children Together (PACT) camps.

A special thanks goes to Dr. Lewis Bender for his work in artfully facilitating the executive retreat and to Dr. Robert Fischer and the Illinois Law Enforcement Executive Institute for their contributions.

Finally, to Dr. Larry Hoover, Dr. Jerry Dowling, and Janice Ahmad, who served as coordinating authors for this book, we convey our appreciation for their energy, talent and commitment.

Thomas J. Jurkanin, Ph.D.

CONTENTS

Page

Foreword .... *xv*
Preface .... *xvii*

Chapter

1. THE POLICE EXECUTIVE'S ROLE 3

2. TEN COMMANDMENTS OF BEING A POLICE EXECUTIVE: RULES OF PERSONAL AND PROFESSIONAL CONDUCT 11

3. LEADERSHIP DEVELOPMENT 31

4. DEPARTMENT MISSION AND INFRASTRUCTURE 43

5. MANAGING THE AGENCY'S CRITICAL COMPONENTS .. 57

6. PLANNING AND BUDGETING: THE ROAD MAP FOR SUCCESS 85

7. EMPLOYEE ASSOCIATIONS 97

8. COMMUNITY-ORIENTED POLICING: FULL SERVICE LAW ENFORCEMENT 107

9. CULTIVATING QUALITY IN POLICING 118

10. POLITICAL REALITIES 128

Bibliography 147
Resources 151
Appendix 153
Name Index 155
Subject Index 156

ENDURING, SURVIVING, AND THRIVING AS A LAW ENFORCEMENT EXECUTIVE

Chapter 1

THE POLICE EXECUTIVE'S ROLE

POLICE AGENCIES ARE UNDOUBTEDLY THE MOST VISIBLE ELEMENT of local government. The media scrutiny is intense and relentless. The very nature of the police role subjects police chiefs and sheriffs to ongoing Monday morning quarterbacking. In a democratic society the police are not trusted, and never will be trusted. Their actions are always subject to scrutiny, and motives are questioned. Given this environment, it is essential that police chiefs and sheriffs grasp the complexity of their role. For example, they are told to acquire the broadest possible input when making administrative decisions. But, a balance must be struck between breadth of input and rapidity of response. Issues arise suddenly in policing, and the public expects a near instantaneous administrative response. Homilies extolling police managers to look before you leap are offset by those such as *he who hesitates is lost*. Agency management is a constant balancing act between expediency and careful planning.

Mintzberg's Managerial Roles

Henry Mintzberg is one of the most popular writers on issues of organizational structure and management today. Mintzberg is not a purveyor of a fad approach characterized by a set of buzz words and clever diagrams. Unlike many of his counterparts, Mintzberg writes about management from an inductive rather than deductive approach.

That is, Mintzberg observes what managers are actually doing with their time and the processes they employ to make decisions, and accurately describes it. Mintzberg takes the perspective that what successful managers do is correct management, not what deductively we might suppose they ought to do.

Employing that perspective, Mintzberg (1989) stipulates three broad managerial roles:

- Interpersonal—figurehead, leader, liaison;
- Informational—monitor, disseminator, spokesperson;
- Decisional—entrepreneur, disturbance handler, resource allocator, negotiator.

The roles are distinguishable, but not necessarily mutually exclusive. While serving as the agency figurehead by making welcoming remarks to a conference, the manager may concurrently be engaging in liaison with persons from related organizations, serving as her/his organizational spokesperson, and disseminating information about the organization. The fact that a manager's role is not easily divided into distinct categories suggests that it is likewise not easily scientifically analyzed. Management is as much an art as a science, according to Mintzberg.

The lack of science in management is nevertheless not well recognized. Organizational theorists are loathe to acknowledge that management may be more art than science. In this respect, several myths exist regarding management, perpetuated by those who insist that management must be a science (Mintzberg, 1989). The myths include:

- A good manager is a reflective calculator.
- Management concentrates on exceptions.
- Managers use information that is systematic and well documented.
- Management is becoming more scientific.

Management is better described as a roller coaster ride through a three-ring circus.

Studies of what managers actually do contradict these myths. First, managers are hardly reflective, systematic calculators when 50 percent of their activities take less than 9 minutes. Managers spend more than 30 minutes on one task only every 2 days, and in 368 observed contacts of managers with other individuals or groups, only 1 could be characterized as general planning. Managers move quickly from one brushfire to the next, and have little time to be reflective. A term born in the 1950s, *organized anarchy,* is the best descriptor.

Observation likewise does not bear out the perception that managers concentrate on exceptions, delegating all routine duties. Managers routinely see between 25 and 50 people, depending upon the organization and the specific management role. The notion that a police chief sees only her/his assistant chiefs below him and the city manager above him, is a myth that every chief or sheriff would recognize. Further, managers spend a great deal of time on ceremonial duties. Ceremonial in this sense is broadly defined, and may include such functions as simply appearing at a patrol shift roll call. The police chief or sheriff is there because he/she "should" be seen by the troops– a ceremonial function. Granted valuable information may be gained by such appearances, but the primary purpose is ceremonial, and it is a routine duty. Further, most problems managers deal with are not big picture issues. They are petty, but symbolically sensitive. Finally, managers find it extremely difficult to delegate many of these so-called routine duties. The totality of use of diverse information essentially prevents delegation. The observation that, "By the time I explain it all, I could do it myself," describes the situation.

It is likewise a myth that managers use information that is systematic and well documented. Managers obtain 80 percent of their information orally. They typically only skim written documents. When was the last time a police chief or sheriff you know sat down and read carefully through a voluminous document? The daily mail is not regarded as a resource of new information, but stuff to be gotten rid of. Importantly, strategic information is typically stale by the time it is written down. Hence, the use of oral information is essential.

Finally, it is a myth that the information age has made management more scientific. Management information reports are not irrelevant, to be sure. But they are only an incremental addition to the information managers already use. Managers describe most decisions as being made using judgment and intuition, not hard data. They are undoubtedly referring in this context to employing a sense of totality of information, including perceptions on organizational culture and an appreciation for organizational history. Computerized data sources cannot convey that totality of perspective.

Nevertheless, information remains the key to effective management. The acknowledgment that formal, written, structured information is not as important as advocates of scientific management would suggest does not negate the importance of information, broadly defined. Managers must have a sense of the political institutions of which they are a part, the community as a whole, the profession of law enforcement, public administration generally, and, last but not least, their own organization. Every decision will be made in that broad context, and the more information a manager has, the better the decisions.

It should be recognized in particular that the role of a chief executive officer, i.e., police chief or sheriff, conveys a status that is unique. Lieutenants and captains will not have the same information access as a law enforcement agency's CEO. The formal authority and status which comes with the role begets information access. Information, in turn, helps secure the authority and status of the CEO position. *Ipso facto*, if a police chief or sheriff fails to obtain information, it may not be obtained at all–simply because subordinates do not have the position, status, or authority to obtain it. Acquiring information is at the core of the role of a law enforcement CEO.

The Evolution of Perspective on Administrative Decision-Making

Information acquisition is only a prerequisite to the truly difficult element of a police executive's role–making hard decisions. No other area of organizational theory has evolved so dramatically in terms of what is viewed as appropriate or correct as decision-making processes. In other segments of organizational theory new perspectives or paradigms normally add to or modify existing perspectives. Thus, in terms of the organization of work, the principles approach added to, but did not replace, scientific management. In turn, the systems approach modified substantially, but did not entirely replace, the principles school. With regard to decision-making, however, current perspectives truly replace and contradict those previously held.

The initial view of what constituted appropriate administrative decision-making was premised upon Weber's ideal bureaucracy (Bolman and Deal, 1997). Max Weber was a nineteenth century German sociologist. In his world, organizations were managed through a process of inherited privilege. He articulated a set of principles for a modern bureaucracy. Although the term "bureaucracy" has become negatively pejorative—with connotations of immovable, complex, stagnated organizations—all of us in fact work in and are dependent upon classic bureaucratic structures. An efficient bureaucracy keeps the trains running on time and is appreciated by both those who work within and who must employ their services.

An important characteristic of Weber's ideal bureaucracy was rational management. The rational manager made decisions exclusively for the benefit of the organization, rather than any personal aggrandizement. Further, the decisions made were premised upon having acquired as much information about the situation as possible, then carefully weighing alternatives, and selecting the best only after being fully informed of all relevant facts. Thus, "good" managers strove to be fully informed before making any decision. We now recognize that this ideal is virtually never achieved.

The principles approach to administrative decision-making, exemplified by administrative books written roughly between 1930 and 1950, depict the manager as an orchestra conductor. Like an orchestra conductor a good manager was idealized as achieving balance in an organization, dedicating a portion of each day's time to various elements of organizational coordination. Most managers at one time or another in an administration course memorized the pneumonic POSDCORB—*P*lanning, *O*rganizing, *S*cheduling, *D*irecting, *CO*ordinating, *R*eviewing, *B*udgeting. Similarly, Henri Fayol's functional approach to management would have the good manager balancing effort among technical, commercial, financial, security, accounting, and managerial elements of organizational coordination. The principles approach viewed the manager as still attempting to achieve Weber's ideal of being fully informed before making any decision. However, the balance overlay was added, i.e., a manager should be careful not to focus excessively on any one element of organizational operations.

In his classical work, *Administrative Behavior* (1945), Herbert Simon articulated a more sophisticated view of administrative decision-making. Simon listed three categories of decision-making situations. The first he termed "objective rationality," in which a manager had total and complete knowledge of the situation and made a decision solely premised upon maximizing organizational values. The second type of situation was that described by the term "subjective rationality," in which a manager made a decision with only partial knowledge, but still attempted to maximize organizational values. Simon speculated that by far the more common situation was described by the term "bounded rationality," in which there is a sequential search for solutions to organizational problems, with managers stopping whenever they find those that are merely satisfactory.

During the 1950's Simon's work evolved. In Marsh and Simon's *Organizations* (1958), the terms "satisficing" and "organized anarchy" were introduced. Satisficing describes the process of bounded rationality, but characterizes it as unacceptable. Organizations that engaged in satisficing never maximized or optimized. That doesn't mean that they might not be successful, only that they are not as successful as they otherwise might be. Marsh and Simon also described the world of management by the term "organized anarchy." It was recognized for the first time that managers are not careful, thoughtful, contemplative planners systematically gathering information before ever making a decision. Rather, the world of the manager is described as hectic and demanding. The contrasting terms "organized" and "anarchy" are deliberatively used to convey the message that managers are not irrational—they attempt to organize their decision-making processes—but have limited ability to do so. Every police chief or sheriff will testify to the hectic reality of their role.

Lindbloom's classic work *The Science of Muddling Through* (1959) describes this process in the world of public administration. Lindbloom noted that managers in the public sector, in addition to facing all the problems prevalent in the private sector, are buffeted by constantly changing political winds. Again, there is the clever use of contrasting terms, "science" and "muddling through." Lindbloom's perspective evolved to a current view of management decision-making—logical incrementalism.

Logical incrementalism describes administrative decision-making as a blend of formal analysis, organizational culture, and politics. In this more realistic view of management decision-making, managers do their best in a chaotic world. The perspective recognizes that while organizational goals might be reasonably clear, organizational objectives are not. In the world of policing, we might by extension note that crime prevention is a recognized and laudable goal. Whether that translates to departmental participation in D.A.R.E. or G.R.E.A.T.

programs is not necessarily clear. Whether under the auspices of crime prevention public police agencies ought to monitor private alarm systems is even less clear.

In this type of environment, managers, in particular public managers, are likely to engage in organizational development incrementally. Absent extreme pressure, risk-taking is measured. One step at a time is favored over organizational revolution. Further, there will be a pattern and logic to organizational development but not necessarily a carefully orchestrated, precisely balanced effort that might be described by the principles approach to management. Changing political winds are taken into account, and constant adjustments are made.

Logical incrementalism is regarded as healthy for most enterprises. More dramatic approaches may be needed in times of crisis. In the private sector, an organization facing potential bankruptcy is not necessarily well served by incremental change. In the public sector, a police agency coming off a major scandal is likewise not necessarily well served by incrementalism. But for the vast majority of organizations the vast majority of the time, logical incrementalism is appropriate. Logical incrementalism is not the equivalent of satisficing. Satisficing can lead to stagnation, failure to adjust to a changing environment, or complacency in a competitive marketplace. Incrementalism embraces change, not stagnation. But organizational development under incrementalism does not require turning the organization upside down every two years. A critical element of a progressive police executive's role is ascertaining the appropriate pace of change.

Antidotes for Satisficing

Police executives should be wary of "cure-all" management fads. But they should not reject every new management perspective. Sometimes what is labeled as a "management fad" can more appropriately be regarded as an effort to combat the tendency of organizations to drift to a satisficing mode. Among such efforts over the last twenty years is management by objectives, planning–programming–budgeting systems, organizational development, zero-based budgeting, reinventing the corporation/government, and total quality management (TQM). From one cynical perspective, none of these efforts have or will stand the test of time. That is, they have their day in the sun, flood the racks at airport bookstores, and fade away. The latest approach, **TQM**, is already fading. But there is a kinder view. What all of these approaches have in common is the institutionalization of organizational change. That is, they are an approach to forcing organizations to systematically and constantly endeavor to optimize rather than satisfice. Each of the efforts is imbued with its own set of buzz words. Each is characterized by sets of clever diagrams, now conveyed pervasively in PowerPoint® presentations. Each has its list of "gurus" commanding $30,000 per appearance speaker fees. And each is greeted by the vast majority of individuals who do the line work in organizations by the attitude that "This, too, will pass." Much of the cynicism is justified. Indeed, this year's set of buzz words and "change diagrams" will indeed pass. But a police manager needs to recognize that a sustained effort to develop an organization is required from its administration. People in any organization are quick to recognize a caretaker leader, and they will respond appropriately. A police chief or sheriff who thrives doesn't have to adopt this year's organizational development buzz words, but he/she must constantly convey a sense of growth and development.

Chapter 2

TEN COMMANDMENTS OF BEING A POLICE EXECUTIVE: RULES OF PERSONAL AND PROFESSIONAL CONDUCT

THE POSITION AS THE EXECUTIVE OF A LAW ENFORCEMENT AGENCY has many responsibilities and rewards. As such, the head of the agency is expected to set the tone of the organization and demonstrate exemplary personal and professional behavior. Subordinates look to the chief executive to establish acceptable behavior standards. Community members continuously monitor the chief's behavior to determine if he/she is the type person they want as the leader of the agency that protects the people and upholds the Constitution and the laws of the land. Early in one's administration, the law enforcement chief executive must clearly articulate the ground rules that he/she has established for the agency and the penalty for violating those rules. This will set the ethical standards of the agency.

Becoming chief executive is a major accomplishment in the chief's career and offers an opportunity to provide uniform, fair and consistent professional service to her/his subordinates, government officials and community residents. This professional service, including ethical standards, is based upon the chief's basic work ethic, beliefs and moral order that he/she has developed and that was influenced through past experiences, including her/his immediate and extended family, schools attended, faith practiced, colleagues, friends and mentors. The community's characteristics and reputation also impact the ethics, principles and beliefs set for the agency.

Professionalism and ethical behavior, being a good person and doing what is right are important for the law enforcement executive to possess and demonstrate to agency members and the community. The purpose of this chapter is to explore ten rules of personal and professional conduct that are vital to the success of a law enforcement executive. These commandments are:

1. Practice what you preach
2. A day's pay for a-day-and-a-half work
3. Maintain and promote integrity
4. Develop a positive image
5. Remain committed
6. Be respectful and you will be respected
7. Accept assistance from others
8. Be eager for knowledge
9. Maintain a healthy lifestyle
10. Set personal goals

Each of these will be discussed separately, as well as the consequences of unethical behavior.

Commandment 1–Practice What You Preach

The chief or sheriff leads by example and if he/she wants agency members to act with integrity in all matters, then he/she must do so first. The old adage "actions speak louder than words" comes to mind when talking about this commandment. Lip service is only that. The chief or sheriff must always be a professional, lead by example, and act the way he/she wants others to act.

The chief executive sets the tone of the organization and its interaction with the community. If he/she is open to subordinates and community members, then the employees will act in the same manner. This is extremely important as police agencies become more customer focused and community-oriented.

Many police chiefs and sheriffs would say that they live in glass houses. Everything they do is noted, recorded and filed for possible future reference. This information is then used when needed, either to support the chief executive or, more likely, to overpower or destroy the chief when something goes wrong. The glass house must be spotless and capable of withstanding any stones that might be thrown. The chief must talk the talk and walk the walk of morality, integrity, and honor.

Commandment 2–A Day's Pay For A-Day-And-A-Half Of Work

A law enforcement chief executive cannot expect to meet the agency's objectives and his/her responsibilities in a regular, nine-to-five, forty-hour work week. The chief must put in long hours to accomplish all that needs to be done. During the honeymoon period, the newly appointed chief or elected sheriff must be especially prepared to put in long hours of work, as there is almost an overwhelming amount of work to do during those early months. According to one chief, "you have to be willing to work as hard as if the police department were your own business" (Scott, 1986).

Most law enforcement chief executives have worked their way up the ladder and have done so at the expense of some personal freedoms. Most good managers feel compelled to work extended hours to accomplish agency and personal goals. Some managers are reimbursed or allowed compensatory time for their extra efforts, while others work strictly for the pleasure or for the feeling of the need to "get the job done." None of this properly prepares one for the twelve-hour work day facing a chief or sheriff.

Staff meetings, telephone conversations, luncheon meetings, press conferences, interviews, report reading, and labor negotiations all take place during the day. That leaves the evening for letter and report writing, budget review, reading of professional journals and other publications, attending city council or county board meetings and meeting with civic, parent-teacher, and church groups. The remainder of the chief's or sheriff's time is spent on duties such as being president of the regional police chief's or sheriff's association, chairperson of the gang crime (or other similar) committee and service on the local 911 board. All of these duties and responsibilities account for the law enforcement chief executive working a day and a half for a day's pay.

The chief executive cannot be in her/his office every work day during normal business hours, due to meetings at other locations, attendance at a late night meeting, or for personal reasons. The absence of the chief's vehicle at the department will be noticed by subordinates.

However, if the chief is often at the department during evening and night shifts that, too, will be observed.

A sergeant, lieutenant, or captain can have someone "cover" for him or her. Sometimes it is the chief. However, a chief's absence is conspicuous. No one can completely cover for the chief. It's not just the completion of tasks or the delegation of assignments. An efficient deputy chief or chief deputy can handle these matters. It is the symbolism of being on the job, ready and able to assume command in times of crisis; being available to answer the mayor's, city manager's, or county administrator's phone calls; standing by to see the press or an anxious parent; and being perceived by the troops as a workaholic. This does not mean that tasks should not be assigned and responsibilities delegated, but the chief remains answerable for all decisions made and transgressions executed. The proverbial buck stops with the chief. Decisions must be well thought out.

It is imperative that the chief executive work long hours and do so in an efficient manner. This includes aligning him/herself with competent people to whom he/she can delegate tasks and responsibilities. By doing this, the chief sets an example for her/his subordinates that hard work is valued and rewarded.

Commandment 3–Maintain and Promote Integrity

The promotion and maintenance of integrity in a law enforcement organization is determined by the chief executive's actions and influence. There is no doubt that the person at the top sets the tone of the organization for everything from hours worked to integrity to image. The chief executive leads by example. Everyone is watching his/her performance as "top cop." When it comes to integrity, there is no gray area. As a past law enforcement mentor was fond of pointing out "either you have it, or you don't."

Successful police executives usually enjoy widespread community support, earned by the confidence that the community has in the chief's integrity. As a public authority figure, the police executive has the responsibility to promote honesty and integrity, and to speak out against unethical behavior. The chief or sheriff is always in the "fish bowl," everyday activities are closely watched by citizens and subordinates, and is seen as a reflection of the integrity of the department.

What is integrity? Is the breach of integrity corruption? At what level of behavior does corruption begin? Can a line be drawn between what is acceptable behavior and what is not acceptable behavior (i.e. a free cup of coffee, using the booth and the telephone provided by a fast food restaurant or convenience store, accepting the reward established for solving a crime or for meritorious service, accepting a Christmas or other holiday gift, half-priced meals, discounts on merchandise for personal use, discount on merchandise for police use)? Does community-oriented policing allow for corruption to take hold? Are officers who are assigned to the same beat for a long period of time trained in what is acceptable behavior and how to avoid situations where corruption could occur? Are the officers monitored to identify problems early so that corrective action can be taken? Each of these questions must be addressed by the chief executive to promote the ethical behavior of all employees and establish an agency that is moral and has the respect of the community.

Integrity can be defined as "excellence of character . . . being the same person in public and private, behaving well even when we have no fear of being caught" (Delattre, 1991). Pollock (1994) suggests that a law enforcement officer ask three questions when faced with an ethical consideration: (1) What must police do under the law?; (2) What does departmental policy dictate?; and (3) What do individual ethics dictate? When a person answers these three questions, the dilemma generally resolves itself. The values and principles that a person develops in one area are very similar to those in another area; generally a person is not strongly ethical in one area and immoral in another. For instance, if an officer has a history of inflicting domestic abuse, he/she may also be inclined to use excessive force while on-duty. Not only must integrity be infused in all aspects of a person's being, ethical standards and integrity must permeate all of the agency, from the recruitment process to equipment procurement. Ethical behavior must be taught in basic police training and continue to be emphasized throughout an officer's career, including the Field Training Officer (FTO) program, in-service training, and supervisor/management education. In this way, not only are the most ethical people recruited and hired, but emphasis on moral behavior is continued to ensure that individual members of the agency remain ethical and that as a whole the department is above reproach and maintains the respect of the community.

If integrity does not exist within the agency and employees are not held to high standards of moral behavior, then corruption will occur. Goldstein (1977) defined corruption as "acts involving the misuse of authority by a police officer in a manner designed to produce personal gain for him/herself or for others." This not only includes monetary gain, but also intangibles such as status, influence, power, future support, or services.

There are many contributing factors to corruption including unenforceable laws, organized criminal interests, improper political interference, the nature of police work, and police discretion (Goldstein, 1977). Additionally, some assignments and duties in police work may present more opportunities for corruption than others and allow for the addictive element of corruption to take hold and grow. These can include working undercover assignments, using informants, deceptive interrogation, parking enforcement (especially in large cities where parking is at a premium and affects commerce) and the bidding, or procurement process.

To determine if corruption exists and, if so, the extent of that corruption in the agency, the chief executive must assess the problem. This means discovering existing areas of corrupt behavior as well as the degree of influence that the political arena has over the chief or sheriff (McCarthy, 1977). To determine if a behavior is corrupt, McCarthy (1977) suggests the use of the totality-of-circumstances rule. The question that should be asked is "Was there quid pro quo involved?" Part of this determination will include investigation of corrupters outside the department, which can include those people in the community who consistently appear at police functions, or who have a wide circle of acquaintances within the department. While some of these may be harmless police buffs, others are not. By determining the internal and external influences of corruption, the chief can then take steps to fight corruption and instill his/her ethical standards that department members are expected to meet.

If corruption has been uncovered, the chief executive must address the corruption openly; acknowledge the extent that the corruption exists, both in the department and in society at large; develop community support for confronting the problem; and finally, don't become a zealot in the fight against corruption (Goldstein, 1977). If instances of corruption have been uncovered, then corrective action must be taken and done so based on the particular problem. If no or relatively little corruption has been found the chief must continue to keep ethics and moral behavior at the forefront, as any perceived loss of control or change in philosophy may allow the seeds of corruption to be sown.

In an effort to maintain an ethical agency and to fight corruption, some law enforcement agencies have developed mission and/or value statements that identify the important objectives of the organization. To regulate the behavior of individual employees, many law enforcement agencies have adopted a Code of Ethics (see Chapter Four). This Code is given to every officer upon entry into the department. Many law enforcement agencies prominently display both the agency mission and the Code of Ethics in the lobby and other areas of the agency. The chief, however, may face different ethical dilemmas than the line officer, front-line supervisor, or middle manager. One such area that can be a source of questionable activity and corruption is the procurement process. The process established by local and state laws must be adhered to in order to avoid allegations of unfairness that can lead to civil actions. Areas most likely to produce litigation include dividing large procurements into several small ones in an effort to streamline the process or to use unofficially preferred vendors; sole sourcing; awarding a contract without any competition; emergency procurements; vague requirements in the request; and allotting a short period to complete the proposal (Asner, 1998). Unsuccessful suppliers are beginning to challenge the procurement process and such a protest to the process can suspend the procurement activity until the challenge has been settled. This may result in delays of days, weeks, or months.

Another area that may cause a great deal of stress to the chief executive is the political arena and the control that it asserts on him/her. Chapter 10, "Political Realities," reviews this issue in-depth. A word of warning is, however, appropriate here; the chief must be aware of the political arena and be vigilant not to become mired in such activity.

Everything the chief or sheriff says and does will be remembered by subordinates and community members. The chief's actions may be duplicated by others and no chief wants those actions to reflect adversely on the department. Not only must the chief executive promote and maintain integrity, he/she must be watchful for violations of the ethical rules of the department and act swiftly when they have been breached. Most of all, the chief must constantly strive to meet the ethical standards developed for the agency. In this way, the chief not only provides vocal support of the values, but also demonstrates the ethical behavior expected of members of the department and the community.

Commandment 4–Develop a Positive Image

The chief executive is not only responsible for the integrity of the agency but also the morale of the employees. If department employees are to be upbeat and positive the chief must first display those characteristics.

Police work can be filled with disappointment and failures, causing employees to feel ineffective and become indifferent. The causes may include seemingly unsupportive supervisors and administrators, prosecutors, and judges viewed as too lenient, inadequate resources, and perceived lack of public support. The chief executive must work to counteract these challenges and help officers overcome the disappointments and failures or to understand the issues if they cannot be overcome.

Positive recognition of employees' contributions should be done on a regular basis. This includes individuals, work groups, divisions and units. Recognition should be provided not only for valiant actions but also for improving the quality of life in the community. The annual award ceremony should be meaningful and something for which to strive. Between award ceremonies, continual recognition of officers' contributions to the department and the community must be done. In this way, police work is made more meaningful and employees can overcome the burn-out so often experienced.

The chief or sheriff must be positive and become a coach and cheerleader for her/his employees. By setting realistic expectations of employees and recognizing those who reach and surpass the expectations, the chief can demonstrate that good work and endurance is valued and will be rewarded.

Commandment 5–Remain Committed

The law enforcement executive was hired or elected for her/his experiences, values, and judgments. The chief should be confident of those qualities and use them to establish the goals, mission, and values of the department. Once developed, the chief executive must be committed to their implementation. This may mean taking risks.

Risk taking can prove rewarding by improving services, quality of life and personnel cooperation. However, risk taking does have its dangers, including fallout from subordinates, the city/county manager or mayor, and/or the community. When this occurs, one must examine the challenge, and if the decision was correct, the chief executive must defend the action. However, if something did go wrong, the chief must admit that a mistake was made and take responsibility for the error. The chief and the agency must face failure immediately. The issue should be examined thoroughly and corrections made where needed. Finally, the chief and the department should learn from the mistake and implement new policies or goals to ensure that the mistake is not repeated in the future.

In most instances, the chief can "weather the storm" by taking responsibility and being responsive. There are, however, some storms from which the chief will not be able to recover. If that should occur, the chief will need to do what is best for the agency and him/herself.

Commitment to the goals, values and mission developed by the chief allows her/him to lead and direct the agency. These values and goals should be in the forefront when making decisions and should guide the decision-making process of not only the chief, but all department personnel.

Commandment 6–Be Respectful And You Will Be Respected

The chief or sheriff can earn the respect of the general public, other leaders, employees, board/council members and violators by treating them with respect and in the manner that the chief executive would like to be treated. The chief needs to be fair, firm, concerned, and sincere in all his/her transactions, including the enforcement of rules. It is also important to maintain a safe environment for employees by providing reliable equipment, effective training, and sound support. These actions show that the chief supports her/his employees and should, in turn, earn their respect.

The chief must be prepared to stand up for those employees who have performed admirably or who have made good-faith mistakes. One way to do this is to recognize those who have done outstanding work for the agency and give them credit for their accomplishments. If a good-faith mistake has been made, the chief should not publicly criticize employees, rather the chief should correct the problems internally and quietly. If a few officers have committed a wrongful act the chief should criticize only them, not all employees. In this way the chief should gain and maintain the respect of agency members and the public, as they will see that the chief stands by the values and moral behavior established for the agency and that employees are seen as individuals, not as a whole.

The chief executive must remember that there will always be some people who will vigorously oppose her/him and others who will be the chief's adamant supporters. Obtaining everyone's support is seldom achieved. The chief must continue to promote the values and missions he/she has set for the agency and not compromise him/herself to obtain everyone's support. The chief should aim for service, not success. If this is done, success will follow. This spirit of service and leadership allows the chief to showcase the principles and moral behavior that he/she wants others to exhibit and by respecting others, the chief will be respected.

Commandment 7–Accept Assistance From Others

The law enforcement chief executive has many responsibilities, job tasks, and people with whom to interact. Though life experiences, training, and education have helped to shape the chief's success, he/she cannot do all of what needs to be done by him/herself. Assistance from others must be sought and accepted. The chief, however, remains the final authority in the department as he/she is ultimately responsible to the community. To meet agency and personal goals, the chief executive needs many types of assistance including the command staff; a confidante, mentor or partner; and a higher power.

To successfully institute change and maintain day-to-day operations of the agency, most law enforcement agencies could not operate without some form of participatory management. The chief must decide the amount of authority that is to be shared and then clearly communicate it to the command staff (Scott, 1986). In order to be comfortable sharing authority, the chief must surround the office with well-qualified people who are loyal, ethical and moral. The chief must give members of the command staff roots in strong values and wings in a free mind so that they accomplish the tasks at hand (Braiden, 1992). By surrounding him/herself with quality people, the chief can be confident that the department goals are being achieved in the manner he/she has established. This delegation of real authority should create a sense of ownership by the members of the command staff. If a person takes ownership of a task, an agency and/or a position, then he/she will do the right thing (see Braiden, 1992).

The chief also needs a confidante with whom to share thoughts, ideas, and concerns. This person can be a spouse, partner, mentor, or close colleague. Some chiefs find their spouse or partner a good sounding board, while others have a mentor who is available for consultation. The main requirement of whomever plays this role is that the chief is certain that the discussions will not be shared with anyone else. This allows the chief to talk to someone about the agency and not carry the "problems of the world on his/her shoulders."

Finally, most chiefs have found it important to have spirituality in their lives. They have found that spirituality contributes to the overall persona of the individual and allows them to share their ideas, thoughts and concerns with God or a higher power. Additionally, some chiefs and sheriffs feel that they are serving humankind and it is an extension of their beliefs. Spirituality is seen as a positive force in their lives and that faith contributes to the ability to do the right thing.

Accepting assistance from others will build a teamwork approach to managing and leading the agency. This approach, in turn, will help the chief or sheriff meet the goals and objectives he/she has established.

Commandment 8–Be Eager for Knowledge

A law enforcement chief executive must stay abreast of technology; current events; topics that impact the community; and current management, leadership, and administration trends and issues. A good leader is not only eager to increase her/his own knowledge but also encourages subordinates to do likewise. In this way, the agency will have proactive leadership and the best trained and most knowledgeable officers possible.

The executive must be familiar with the history of the agency and community to understand the past and not repeat mistakes. While the past may explain current circumstances, the chief executive should move forward and make changes based on her/his knowledge about the needs, values, and mission of the department and community.

The executive should also be familiar with the financial aspects of the municipality and be up-to-date on local current events and the impact they may have on policing. For example, a major reduction in local industrial employment or the closing of a major business may significantly alter the types of calls for service the agency receives and, perhaps, the method of providing police service. The chief should also be aware of the changing ideology of the work force. He/she should become knowledgeable about unions and labor relations and their application in the public and private sector. These, too, can affect the way police business is conducted.

The chief executive should employ both formal and informal means of training and education. Resources from organizations such as the Illinois Law Enforcement Executive Institute, the Illinois Association of Chiefs of Police, the Illinois Sheriffs Association, the Illinois Municipal League, and the Illinois Association of County Officials, as well as their national counterparts are invaluable for the chief when implementing her/his training program. Informal learning can take place by subscribing to, reading, and studying law enforcement publications, as well as journals from areas such as technology, management, leadership, and administration. These sources can assist with strategic planning and budget preparation, as well as providing an opportunity to review ideas, trends and successful programs from other communities.

Active membership in local, regional, state and national police organizations will allow the chief or sheriff to develop contacts and exchange information, experiences and knowledge with fellow chiefs and sheriffs. These associations have a rich history of being serious about assisting their members and are tremendous sources of knowledge for police executives. The chief, the department, and ultimately the community benefit as knowledge, talents and abilities are expanded through active membership in these organizations. The executive can begin by contributing time and talent through committee work that will expose the executive to both immediate and future trends in law enforcement and enhance the chief's ability to serve the community. The chief executive should also take advantage of training offered by these organizations.

Technology is in a constant state of change. As faster, less expensive and more powerful equipment and computer software become available, the chief executive must be knowledgeable about its capabilities and how it may assist in the operation of the agency. This does not mean that the chief must become an expert in all of the equipment and applications, rather the chief must possess some fundamental knowledge of the equipment and programs and the department's needs. In addition, the Internet is becoming a source of widely used and useful information. For example, the National Institute of Justice has put all of its publications on-line for downloading by interested parties. This can certainly become a valuable source of information for the law enforcement executive and his/her agency.

The quest for knowledge should also be applied to the programs that have been implemented. Many programs in law enforcement are implemented and continued or eliminated simply on intuition. The chief should encourage, and perhaps even mandate, that the effectiveness of all on-going programs be evaluated and that new programs be instituted only after a needs assessment has been completed. The evaluation and assessment may be as simple as showing an increase in the number of incidents reported (for example, an increase in sexual assaults may inspire an investigator to institute a rape awareness campaign) or as elaborate as a time series survey of the attitudes of graduates of the Citizen Police Academy. The knowledge gained from such an assessment or evaluation can be invaluable in assigning personnel and justifying funding at budget time. Implementation of this process will also provide knowledge to the law enforcement agency concerning the effectiveness of already implemented programs and the need for new programs. Most police officers are by instinct investigators; therefore, this quest for knowledge can provide an additional method to utilize those skills.

The executive should also encourage subordinates to attend training courses and continue their formal education. To accomplish this, the executive must provide the necessary resources. Encouraging and requiring other agency members to participate in training will empower them to take on new duties and responsibilities and allow the department to react to new situations and mandates in a responsible and effective manner. The chief executive can also make informal learning take place in the agency by instituting roll-call training, encouraging reading of police and related materials, Internet access of law enforcement information and encouraging, or requiring, those that have attended training to share the ideas and knowledge gained with their colleagues, either through formally organized training sessions or in roll-call situations. Often, when someone is required to teach what they have learned, additional learning takes place. This can also be a cost effective way of imparting knowledge about critical or topical issues. Many training programs are offered in the train-the-trainer format designed for attendees to teach others the knowledge and information gained. Again, this is a cost effective model and allows officers to be more active in department training.

If the "troops" see the chief actively pursuing training and education, using the knowledge gained from those sessions to improve the department and instill the lessons to others, they will also embrace learning. The encouragement from the head of the organization is often what officers need to continue their education and training and to share it with others. Law enforcement executives can require such training take place so that their agency is responsive to the issues and problems of its community in the new millenium.

Commandment 9–Maintain a Healthy Lifestyle

A person who is physically fit is able to perform and react better than one who is not. As the head of a law enforcement agency the chief executive is expected to work long hours, respond to emergencies, represent the department and set an example for subordinates. If the chief executive is not physically fit and does not promote a healthy lifestyle, not only is her/his health in danger but a precedent is set for agency employees to maintain the same lifestyle. A healthy lifestyle includes annual medical examinations; proper nutrition; maintaining a healthy weight; participating in regular exercise; practicing stress management; avoiding the excessive use of alcohol, tobacco and other drugs; having outside interests and hobbies; maintaining a balance between work, home and other commitments; and having contact with non-law enforcement friends. By incorporating these practices into one's lifestyle, a person can decrease the risk of many of the ten leading causes of death in the United States as listed in Table 2.1.

All adults should have regular medical physical examinations that are age specific and designed for preventative care. The health care provider should recommend those procedures and tests that are most appropriate but at the minimum should include blood pressure, cholesterol testing, prostrate examinations for males over 40 and well woman check ups, including mammograms, for females over 35.

TABLE 2.1

TEN LEADING CAUSES OF DEATH IN THE UNITED STATES

1. Heart Disease
2. Cancer
3. Stroke
4. Chronic Obstructive Pulmonary Disease
5. Accidents
6. Pneumonia/Influenza
7. Diabetes
8. HIV/AIDS
9. Suicide
10. Chronic Liver Disease and Cirrhosis

Source: Center for Disease Control

A medical check up is also necessary if the chief executive is going to start different eating or exercise regimens. The medical physical will allow the health care provider to confirm that the chief is maintaining a healthy lifestyle or suggest changes that need to be undertaken and be done in a safe manner.

Many people would benefit from adopting a healthy diet. The principles of a healthy diet include variety, balance, and moderation. These can be attained by following the United States Department of Agriculture food guide pyramid recommendations. The pyramid provides the daily caloric and nutritional requirements for an average person. Following the guidelines limits fat, sugar, and salt intake. Some adjustments may have to be made to account for age and activity level, as a more active person needs more calories than a sedentary person. It is also important to look for hidden sugar, fat and salt when making food choices, as some foods that are labeled low-fat or fat-free may have excessive sugar in order to retain the flavor of the original product. Included in good nutrition is the consumption of eight 8-ounce glasses of water per day. Substituting a glass of water for coffee or soda during the day will help meet this need.

Making wise eating choices should improve health problems such as high blood pressure and high cholesterol. Maintenance of a healthy weight is another necessary factor for maintaining a healthy lifestyle. Excess weight is an associated risk factor to several of the top ten causes of death. Several weight/height guidelines have been published.

Simple changes in the diet, such as drinking one percent or skim milk instead of whole; using low-fat or fat-free salad dressing instead of regular; using less butter, sour cream and/or cheese on a baked potato; and choosing fish rather than beef can produce weight loss without any noticeable sacrifices. If a weight loss of several pounds is to be undertaken, a medical physical by a health care provider should be completed. This will ensure that the diet plan provides all of the needed nutrients and that the person's health is not put at risk by the eating plan.

Regular physical activity also contributes to a healthy lifestyle, as it helps reduce many of the risk factors associated with the leading causes of death. Exercise also reduces stress and its effects. Regular exercise generally means physical activity that increases the heart rate to 60–80 percent of its maximum for 20–30 minutes, 3 times per week. The exercise program can include walking, jogging, weight lifting, bicycling or other activities that will increase the heart rate. To institute and maintain an exercise program, a person has to be just a little selfish and have commitment to oneself. Time must be scheduled for exercise and not be easily rescheduled. Many law enforcement agencies have fully equipped exercise areas and the chief executive should take advantage of this arrangement. If this is not available, the executive may want to join a health or exercise facility or use the track at the local high school or university. Anyone who begins an exercise program is advised to first see a health care provider. A trainer can also be consulted to devise an exercise plan that is tailored to the person's fitness level and health needs.

The chief executive of a law enforcement agency may be under a lot of stress due to the many expectations placed on the position, both from within and outside the department. A healthy lifestyle includes the institution of a stress management program. Selye (1976), a well-known stress researcher, defines stress in the medical sense as the "rate of wear and tear on the body." Stress can be both good (eustress) i.e., a job promotion, or bad (distress) such as when a loved one dies. The body physiologically responds the same to both types of stress, however the longer the stressor remains and the greater the degree of the stressor, the more likely a person will experience ill effects from the stress. The introduction of a stressor to a person immediately causes a rise in blood pressure, the secretion of sweat, and an increased heart rate. If the stress is allowed to continue, irritability; hyper-excitation;

depression; emotional instability; inability to concentrate; fatigue; bruxism; excessive alcohol use; and other behavioral conditions may result (Selye, 1976). These conditions are also associated with many of the leading causes of death.

In order to prevent stress from accumulating and causing health and psychological problems, the chief executive must manage the stress to reduce its effects. The first step is recognition of the stressors in one's life. Often the employee assistance program in a jurisdiction sponsors formal stress management workshops where identification of stressors can be done. Health insurance companies sometimes offer workshops or questionnaires that can be used to assess the stress in one's life. It is suggested that contact be made with these agencies or a health care provider to obtain assistance to identify the stressors. The next step is to practice stress management everyday. Some people find exercise a great stress reducer, in addition to the other health benefits it provides. Other people participate in a hobby, such as photography, gardening, or woodworking. Still others find relaxation exercises and meditation to be effective. No matter which techniques are used to reduce stress, they must be relaxing and take one's mind away from the stressors.

Another important aspect for maintaining a healthy lifestyle is the avoidance of the excessive use of tobacco, alcohol and other drugs. The health risks associated with the use of smoking tobacco are well-known. Less well-known are the health risks associated with non-smoking or chewing tobacco, including gum disease and cancer of the mouth and throat. Use of any tobacco product should be stopped. There are several products on the market to assist in smoking cessation and, again, health care providers should be consulted prior to the usage of these products.

Alcohol abuse has contributed to the downfall of many law enforcement leaders. Its abuse may start as a source of relief from the pressures and stressors of the job; however, it just does not solve the problem. Alcoholism is among the greatest dangers to a stressed-out chief or sheriff. The danger is especially strong since these administrators, as community leaders, are often expected to attend those mandated, but quasi-social functions where the first order of business is a trip to the bar. This danger is compounded by the occasional travel requirements that take a chief out of the home jurisdiction and beyond the "fish bowl." It can be a relief to be temporarily excused from chief-like protocols and exemplary behavior, but the relief is often accompanied by temptations that can range from public intoxication to infidelity. Needless to say, the momentary exhilaration is sure to be followed by a degree of controversy that can ruin careers and destroy marriages. Unlike battle scars, the wounds from personal embarrassment will seriously weaken the chief or sheriff, both inside and outside the department.

A cocktail or glass of wine at a restaurant while eating dinner is perceived differently than sitting at the restaurant's bar, "slugging them down." However, when driving a vehicle, whether a company or personal one, consumption of alcohol should be avoided. Many municipalities have policies against the operation of a company vehicle after consuming alcohol, and this policy includes the chief executive. If an accident occurs, the chief will have to answer to a wide array of officials and citizens, whether he/she was at fault or not. Additionally, if the chief or sheriff supports the work of organizations such as Mothers Against Drunk Driving (MADD) and Students Against Drunk Driving (SADD), it becomes that much more important to "practice what you preach."

The use of over-the-counter and prescription drugs should be carefully monitored. Many individuals have become addicted to such legal drugs. These too can create as much damage to one's career as alcohol.

The chiefs executive's use of tobacco, alcohol and other drugs will be closely monitored by both those inside and outside the department. The chief's use of these substances not only determines the type of person he/she is but also sets the tone of acceptance for department employees and community residents. Most law enforcement agencies have policies concerning the use of these substances and the chief or sheriff is also expected to conform.

The last factor concerning the maintenance of a healthy lifestyle is having outside interests and hobbies; maintaining a balance between work, home and other commitments; and having contact with non-law enforcement friends. The chief must be able to carve out time for family and his/her private life. This may mean making and keeping social commitments, except for emergencies, with family and those who are dear.

All of the elements of a healthy lifestyle are important aspects of being a well-rounded individual and being physically and psychologically fit. They will not only keep the chief healthy but will also set an example for his/her subordinates.

Commandment 10—Set Personal Goals

Those who rise to the top have done so through hard work and the realization of goals set earlier in her/his career. As the chief or sheriff, one has probably reached their career goal, that of being "top cop." Having attained this objective, it is now time to reassess career and personal goals.

The review of goals should include short, medium, and long-term objectives, as well as an assessment of skills already possessed and those that need development. Being chief or sheriff may require different skills and strategies than those used in previous positions; therefore it is necessary to examine personal strengths and limitations as they relate to this role. This review and the goals established can help the chief executive establish the future direction not only of him/herself, but also the direction the agency will take under her/his command.

In addition to career goals, personal goals should also be reexamined. As one's career progresses or changes, so, too, does one's personal life. The goals established earlier may need to be modified, including the examination of retirement and personal financial planning.

The need for an assessment of personal and career goals is important at this juncture of a police executive's life. Having attained the position at the top, the goals and objectives developed for this role and beyond should serve the chief well in establishing a roadmap for him/herself and for the department.

Conclusion

A public office is a public trust. No person is expected to be infallible; indeed, to suppose that anyone can be infallible in the conduct of public or private life is arrogant and dangerous. The public trust, rather, calls for "good intentions" and the very best exertions (George Washington, 1796).

The chief or sheriff is expected to set the tone of the organization and demonstrate exemplary personal and professional behavior. This can be accomplished by adopting rules of personal and professional conduct and developing a moral code that agency members are expected to follow.

The chief executive is top cop and everything he/she does is examined, sometimes copied and sometimes recorded to be used later as needed. The chief executive does live in a glass house, but by being ethical and moral the chief can withstand the many rocks that will be thrown. The chief should be the first to provide uniform, fair and consistent professional service to his/her employees and to the community. The ten rules of personal and professional conduct should serve the law enforcement executive well, both for self growth and in establishing the expected behavior of department members.

Chapter 3

LEADERSHIP DEVELOPMENT

LEADERSHIP SKILLS AFFECT every managerial function. Leadership is distinguishable from management; leadership includes vision. As stated by the former Chief of Police of Champaign, Illinois, Donald Hanna, in his book, *Police Executive Leadership,* "looking into the future in only one direction has a consequence of visionary blindness." Police executives who wish to exercise visionary leadership must scan the horizon. How accurately do they anticipate changes and expectations? How responsive are police practices to these changes and expectations? How committed are the police to modify practices consistent with these changes and expectations in order to grow and thrive (not just survive) in our environment?

For leadership to occur, there must exist a sense of loyalty, confidence and pride among the leader, those who follow and those who are served. To lead, leaders must gain insight into themselves. That means truly thinking through, "Who am I, what am I about?" Leadership requires being aware of one's own values, expectations, feelings and reactions. Attributes associated with leadership include communication skills, integrity, management ability, and negotiation acumen. In comparison, technical knowledge plays a less important role.

In this respect, a chief or sheriff should not strive to be "super-cop." It is not the law enforcement administrator's duty to be out front, riding the "streets" with the officers. Leadership in law enforcement organizations is certainly made easier if the administrator has a track record of operational experience. Police managers should stay in touch with "the street." But an effective law enforcement leader is an effective administrator. Contact with operations should be done to assure managerial relevance, not to substitute patrol and investigations for administration.

The same balance should be maintained in community and media relations. Selectively making community appearances and spending time addressing neighborhood groups, special interest groups and political interests can hold a law enforcement executive in good stead when the time comes for problem-solving and/or explaining why particular law enforcement actions were necessary. The police executive who has created the perception/reality of community involvement and accessibility will do far better in riding out the inevitable storms arising from policing a democracy. But external communication must be balanced with internal management. It is incumbent upon the chief or sheriff to inspire his employees so that they may achieve their individual potential. This requires time.

Perceptions are important when a chief or sheriff attempts to establish a "hands-on" management style. Implementing a "management by walking around" style gives the administrator an informal view of departmental operations. This style also creates the perception that the chief has knowledge of all areas of the department and does not manage from behind the desk in the "big" office. The selective use of this style will not detract from the administrative management of the department and will contribute significantly to the way the officers view their top administrator.

It is important to recognize and remember the image, influence, and power of the police chief or sheriff. Leading by example sets the tone for the position, and in turn, the agency. The person who is CEO should display pride, quality service and integrity. But these qualities are largely invisible inside the chief's office. Contact with employees is essential.

Competing Constituencies

Increasingly, police chiefs must deal with, and strike a balance among, an ever increasing number of competing and sometimes antithetical constituencies. Balancing interests within a community is not a new role for police executives. What is different is the number of competing groups and the intensity of their demands on police. The competing constituencies can range from unions that want more leave time for officers to community groups that want greater contact with police personnel (clearly impossible if police personnel are absent on leave). Competing groups can include Mothers Against Drunk Driving versus bar and restaurant owners who assert that overactive enforcement stifles and undermines their business profits. Competing forces such as these frequently conspire to produce a political environment that makes it seem impossible for a police executive to succeed. Rigid regulation of alcohol service can be the catalyst for political action on the part of restaurant owners. Lack of enforcement can stimulate political action by anti-drinking groups.

The chief's or sheriff's role is thus very different than that of their assistants. Although duties will be identical to assistants' positions with respect to most management, the chief or sheriff must participate in the political arena. Balance to maintain equilibrium between the internal organization and the external political environment is difficult.

Professional police administrators must make decisions routinely that alienate some members of the community. The nature of the job precludes a chief or sheriff from making "win-win" decisions every time. Through no fault of their own, tenure for police chiefs is often very short. But politically unpopular decisions are less likely to result in job loss if community involvement is maintained. The words "politically popular" may not sound consistent with unbiased, professional law enforcement. But those who believe that politics has no place in law enforcement usually find themselves frustrated, neutralized and eventually dismissed from their jobs.

Time Management

Time management is essential for success. Time management is an important tool in accomplishing tasks, increasing performance and reducing stress. All too often distractions shift the direction in which the chief moves at any particular time. A written agenda or schedule is a plan, a map of where to go that day. After any distraction, a simple review of the plan or map will realign tasks and bring focus back to priorities or goals.

A CEO should encourage scheduled meetings or appointments,

discouraging "walk-in" visits. It is often necessary to allow screening of calls or visitors. The secretary or clerk should be briefed on what calls to refer, what calls are important to pass on and when the chief or sheriff will be available to receive visitors. Balance is, of course, necessary. The community is a valuable asset. The chief or sheriff who becomes too difficult to reach may acquire a reputation for being unresponsive. A chief or sheriff must keep himself/herself available whenever possible.

Mentorship

Usually the first mentors in chiefs' careers were the field training officers who took them under their wing. As they gained experience, others no doubt also helped them grow. To have the active interest of a mentor is wonderful. Mentors come from many relationships–parents, extended family, teachers, professors, neighbors, fellow workers, supervisors. Typically, mentors are "a generation ahead." Police managers should not forget them, but thank them often for contributing to their success.

It is natural for a chief or sheriff to want to "pay back" for the mentoring received in his/her career. Administrators unconsciously look for persons who have talent, demonstrate good work ethics and values, have a willingness to learn, and are willing to accept suggestions, direction and constructive criticism. As long as it does not degenerate to favoritism, mentorship is a healthy part of management development.

Delegating

Delegation is a strength of leadership. A CEO should have the confidence to assign tasks to others and expect that they will do the job right, delegating to others tasks of real responsibility. Generally, delegation establishes confidence and encourages motivation in people. Further, employees today do not accept an autocratic work environment. Since the advent of such principles as quality circles, team management, participatory management and team building, employees demand to have policy input. However, employees still look for guidance and direction. A laissez-faire style of management generally is viewed by personnel as symptomatic of a weak executive, and their level of confidence in the boss' competence will be diminished.

Team building is essential. Each employee has the ability to contribute. Final authority is with the chief or sheriff, but employees should become part of the planning and policy development process. Delegation of responsibility and the authority to perform a function is an important motivator.

Delegation must be accompanied by authority and responsibility. The authority comes as an extension of the chief or sheriff and empowers the employee to perform tasks without interference. Responsibility charges the employee to get the job done. Of course, tasks such as meeting with members of the city/county government or appearing before the media on critical issues may be areas in which delegation is inappropriate.

In his book, *Managing Management Time*, William Oncken wrote of work-related initiatives as being viewed as:

1. Do it, and don't inform me. (full authority to act)
2. Do it, but let me know what you are doing. (full authority with accountability)
3. Do it only upon my approval. (limited authority)
4. Do not do it. (no authority)

Oncken goes on to say these delegated initiatives will vary according to situation.

Policy Manuals

Every police department should have a carefully developed set of policies, procedures, rules, and regulations. They are a part of the formal directive system. Regardless of what the department calls them, they need to be up-to-date. Simple definition of the terms are:

Policies: What we do—a guideline,
Procedures: How we do it,
Rules or regulations: Specific and restrictive directions with no exceptions.

Policies and procedures are not written in stone; they can and should evolve. If deviation from policy routinely occurs, the policy should probably be modified.

Rules and regulations are written to be enforced and should not change unless they become outdated due to case law, state statutes, or other legislation. Violation of rules usually causes disciplinary action to occur. A police manager should make sure rules are heeded and when they are violated, take action. Probably the best approach is to review all critical policies, procedures, and regulations every six months for any update. All others are reviewed on a yearly basis. These reviews should be documented and kept current.

Sometimes policies, procedures, rules, and regulations are so out-of-date that they must be totally rewritten. If they are rewritten, a draft copy should be distributed for review. Even though it may take longer, this is the best method to get everyone involved, to get a departmental "buy-in," and to get a plan that is accepted by the people who do the job or enforce the law.

If the need for a written procedure is critical, it may have to be written quickly and put in to effect immediately. Later it can be reviewed and altered. It is a good practice to have a legal review. Sometimes a single word can make a difference in litigation. Another concern is to ensure that the procedure does not violate any labor contract provisions. After policies, procedures, rules and regulations are written, all employees should be trained, especially supervisors, regarding application. Procedures are of no use if employees don't understand or abide by them.

Communication Skills

Good communication relates both ideas and emotions. Communication is developmental and can be inspirational. Betty Morgan, author of the book, *Managing Communications for Productivity*, writes, "Inherent in individuals is a basic need for intimacy with those people who are perceived as significant in their life. In business, industry or in any institution where people are required to produce goods or services in order to earn their livelihoods, relationships between co-workers assume a high degree of significance, perhaps disproportionate to their true worth and identity. These relationships are established, maintained, and can be enhanced through communication." The ability to gain loyalty and generate motivation is dependent upon ability to form relationships using communication.

Personal attention is also part of the dynamics of communication. CEOs should try to remember important dates–birthdays, anniversaries–and other important personal information–names of employee's spouse and children. It may sound a little patronizing, but it lets each employee know that they are a "real person" to the CEO, not just a cog in the wheel.

Informal Organization Structure

Every organization has both a formal and informal structure. The formal structure is well defined, usually published as the organizational chart. Organizational charts are usually built pyramid style with the command staff on top, and authority cascading down through all units to the police officer. In police agency formal organization, quasi-military terms are used to denote hierarchy, including chain-of-command, unity of command and span of control. In times of emergency and normal operations, the formal structure is important to the safe and efficient operation of the organization. However, it is often bypassed. The informal structure is never formally recognized, but the chief of police or sheriff must know its dynamics.

The informal structure is typically premised upon personality. Informal leaders are usually non-supervisors with long tenure on the department. They are typically intelligent, hard-working and loyal employees of the department. In their role they hopefully have the good of the organization in mind. However, this is not always the case; some are very self-serving. A good chief of police or sheriff should know the abilities of these leaders and know how to use them for the benefit of the organization.

It is necessary in any organization to ensure communications flows both vertically and horizontally. Some issues are properly handled through the formal chain of command. On the other hand, many day-to-day activities and decisions get "bottle-necked" in the bureaucratic chain when a more informal method could and should be used. Getting something accomplished is the first requisite. Whether procedure or protocol was followed is secondary. Supervisors should be encouraged to cross divisional lines when appropriate to solve problems.

So called "open door policies" by definition by-pass formal chain-of-command. A police administrator needs to define any "open-door policy." Does it really mean "come on in anytime?" Or, does it mean the door is only open at certain times and only with prior permission. There have been instances where an employee has been chastised by an immediate supervisor because he/she used an open-door policy as it was published by the chief of police or sheriff. It should be understood that a chief of police is accessible by appointment. Unless it is a highly sensitive matter, reasons for the meeting should be explained.

Developing Community Influence

The leadership role of a police chief or sheriff requires one to broaden community association. This builds an influence base supporting the responsibilities of a chief or sheriff. Everyone in the community, from newborns to senior citizens, are part of this responsibility. Senior citizens in particular are among the best supporters of sound professional law enforcement.

Relationships also need to be developed with management peers from the village/city/county being served. This includes persons who hold key positions within the fire service, public works, parks, finance, and other leaders from other criminal justice agencies, such as the presiding judge, court personnel and state's attorney office. Communication with all of these is part of professional networking.

Community expectations legitimately place demands upon a police agency. The needs of communities, though similar in character, do vary significantly. Priorities in particular vary substantially. All groups within any community have a role in determining the law enforcement priorities of that community. It is necessary for the police administrator to develop a network in which the various groups can communicate their views. What governs the priorities of the department should depend on what the members of the community determine these priorities to be. Successful performance by a department as a service agency is determined by the community's belief that the agency is responsive.

Developing Personnel and Supervisors

In most police departments, supervisors are selected by traditional written civil service tests. Although reading lists may contain books addressing supervisory skills, additional training should be provided. The officer promoted to sergeant takes on a position that is probably the most difficult in any police agency. It is a giant step from being "one of the guys" to being the "boss," and certainly is not an easy one. A new sergeant is usually ill-prepared to tackle the role change without proper training. In some departments it is a practice to send all newly-promoted sergeants to staff and command school. They are a worthwhile investment for the officer and the department. Training should not stop with completion of a staff and command school. In-service training addressing decisionmaking, leadership skills, policy making, and proper disciplinary skills is important.

LIABILITY TRAINING. Vicarious liability training is a must for police agencies (see Chapter 5). Proper training in this area will assist the supervisor in making correct decisions. It should be given by an experienced attorney on at least an annual basis. Laws and court decisions are changing at a fast pace and supervisors need to be up-to-date on liability matters. The expense to train officers and supervisors is a mere pittance compared to the millions of dollars that can be spent on vicarious liability litigation.

ROLL CALL TRAINING. The roll call (the ten–fifteen minute period prior to going on duty) represents an excellent opportunity to provide updated information in a compact, comprehensive manner. The mistakes many police administrators make when designing roll call training are:

- Failure to provide "train-the-trainer" instruction to the roll-call instructors.
- Failure to allow the sergeants (typical roll-call instructors) and line officers to "buy into" policy and procedure development.
- Failure to condense the information into manageable increments for delivery.
- Failure to utilize available visual aids and new technology such as computer-based training.
- Failure to ensure understanding and retention by line officers.

A roll call training program requires planning and investment. At the same time it contributes substantially to the creation of an atmosphere of continuous improvement.

MEETINGS. Department meetings are usually seen only as a vehicle for gaining input for policy and procedure development. But they also represent an opportunity for leadership development. Administrators leading meetings should have some facilitator training or actual facilitator assistance. Department meetings allow all members of the staff to develop a sense of "ownership" in how the department is operated. In and of itself, this is a form of personnel development.

TEAM BUILDING. Team building can be integrated into any type of departmental structure. Although team building is best developed in a community policing orientation, the philosophy can be embraced in the most militarily structured departments. Teams can be built around squads, shifts, job classifications, and/or functions. Once identified, teams must be involved in goal-setting, defining processes, and then recognized for achievement.

Team building is a top-down, bottom-up philosophy that must be nurtured through participation and rewards. Police departments are beginning to redefine individual performance goals, moving away from the traditional "numbers" approach to one of achievement of mutually defined objectives. Team input is central to this process. Officers involved in community-oriented policing can consider themselves on the "cutting edge" of redefining performance objectives in terms of identifying new measures of evaluating the success of their program.

STAFFING ALLOCATION. Proper staffing of an organization is essential for providing both timely services to the public and personnel development. Proper staffing does not come from a "seat of the pants" approach but from structured planning. Factors requiring consideration include how the community is geographically structured—whether there are major highways, commercial developments, manufacturing complexes or residential areas that divide the community. An isolated portion of the community may necessitate more resources simply to keep response times reasonable. Likewise, a neighborhood that is largely residential will create more activity on an around-the-clock basis than a manufacturing area.

Population will also dictate human resource requirements, but not necessarily on a formula basis. An *a priori* ratio of officers per thousand population is no longer regarded as an appropriate means to determine human resource needs. The history of the type, time, and number of calls remain important. However, proactive community policing initiatives must also be considered.

SPECIALIZED UNITS. Beyond the smallest agencies there is a need for specialized units to accomplish the goals of crime prevention and apprehension. Specialization occurs in investigations, narcotics, traffic, juvenile, community relations, and tactical operations. Many departments are also involved in regional specialized units such as Metropolitan Enforcement Groups (MEG), federal drug units and state drug and investigations units.

Assignment of personnel to specialized functions must be carefully done. The method used must be consistent to avoid favoritism allegations. Information should be gathered from personnel files, evaluations, the individual's supervisor and from those currently in the unit with the vacancy. A rotation system is advisable so that upwardly mobile officers can feel they have a chance to be transferred into one of the special units.

A chief or sheriff should never send someone to a regional unit because they would like to get rid of them for a couple of years. Every officer is an ambassador from the department to the regional unit. Personnel from other agencies in regional units will judge the professionalism of the department based upon the individuals assigned.

PHYSICAL FITNESS. Posted clearly on the gymnasium wall at the Illinois State Police Academy is a sign which simply states "When you choose law enforcement, you give up the right to be unfit." Unfortunately, experience has shown that the emphasis on fitness by the organization and the individual diminishes after the basic training period. Few will argue that there is not a direct correlation between individual fitness and on-duty injuries and self-sickness. Unfit officers generate excessive workers compensation and disability costs.

Physical fitness is an individual issue and no organizational policies, rules or directives can force an individual to become or remain fit. Departments that have tried find themselves in conflict with applicable federal and state laws that provide job protection to employees. However, the benefits of exercise, good nutrition and a healthy lifestyle are beginning to become a part of the police culture. Fortunately the current generation is more health conscious than the last.

Traditional mandatory methods of establishing fitness are being replaced by voluntary "positive" fitness programs. Usually linked to annual physical fitness medical examinations, these programs provide insurance premium reduction incentives with achievement of preestablished standards of weight, cholesterol and non-smoking.

Some programs encourage family members to participate in nutrition and wellness seminars.

Sheriffs Special Concerns

Accessibility is extremely important for an elected official. As a public official, the sheriff must be present and available to department employees, county officials, state officials and the public. It will be tempting to always be available, as was the case when campaigning. However, giving due regard to internal administrative issues prevents full accessibility. Guidelines should be established and will vary with the size of the jurisdiction. The guidelines should ensure that the sheriff can be reached regardless of the position or the station of the person seeking accessibility. However, accessibility must also reflect the demands on the sheriff's time. For example, in one county there is a citizen who calls to speak with the sheriff several times a week. However, one brief conversation on an occasional basis will satisfy her. This practice does not take much valuable time, and she is happy that her call was answered.

Chapter 4

DEPARTMENT MISSION AND INFRASTRUCTURE

Mission and Strategy

IT IS DIFFICULT TO DEVELOP A REASONABLY SIMPLIFIED STATEMENT of the police mission. Clearly, it is not mere enforcement of criminal statutes. Certainly law enforcement is a common denominator among innumerable police activities, in fact the majority of police activities. But delivering death messages has nothing to do with law enforcement, standing by downed wires until a power company arrives has nothing to do with law enforcement and many of the dispute resolution activities in which the police engage are at best tangentially related to law enforcement.

Thus, we end up substituting very broad descriptors of the police mission, for example, public service. The problem here is that these terms become so broad as to be meaningless. The terms don't really distinguish the police role from the functions of government generally or offer any criteria for sorting the governmental functions that should be the purview of the police department from those that are the responsibility of other governmental agencies. Our best efforts tend to result in mission statements that are actually a list of ten to fifteen different functions, hardly a mission statement. Nevertheless, it is the perception of mission that most influences police professionals in their choice of strategy. Unfortunately, differences in such perceptions are not well articulated. Most discussions of mission never move beyond, "It's clearly not mere law enforcement, so how about 'to protect and serve?'" The lack of clearly defined mission boundaries leaves us wandering all over the map when strategy is discussed.

The overwhelming majority of private sector organizations operate within a narrowly defined sector of the economy. Indeed, the flurry of corporate acquisitions and mergers that occurred on Wall Street during the early 1980s, assembling conglomerates of unrelated enterprises under the umbrella of a single "financial corporation," disintegrated. The sixth principle of Peters and Waterman's *In Search of Excellence* (1982)– "*stick to the knitting*"– was proved valid. Those companies that stick to the business they know prosper best in the long run. And indeed, even the icon of diversity in American business, Sears, Roebuck and Company, has recently seen its percentage of the retail sales market slip steadily, particularly to the onslaught of a small retailer from Arkansas who initiated a chain that initially focused on the needs of small towns in America, reminiscent of the specific mission of Sears, Roebuck and Company of one hundred years ago.

Serving largely unrelated objectives is a difficult posture to maintain successfully for any organization. It can be accomplished for a period of time, occasionally even for an extended period of time. But organizations with diffuse missions tend to be both the exception and short lived.

In the public sector it is only the police that we ask to maintain such a posture. Other governmental agencies have a clearly focused mission, or at least a clearly focused central mission. For example, no one questions the mission of fire departments. They do take responsibility for some services ancillary to fire fighting. Since fire departments have to handle hazardous materials whenever they respond to an industrial fire, in most jurisdictions by extension they have been made responsible for hazardous materials problems wherever they occur in a community. In some communities fire departments also handle emergency medical services (EMS) response. Again, however, this is an extension of fire fighter responsibilities on the fire ground, and the dispersion of fire stations throughout a community makes them a natural base for stationing ambulances. The clear central mission of every fire department, however, remains fire prevention and suppression.

Further, when one moves beyond our sister public safety agency, mission statements are even more tightly focused. Departments of sanitation, public works, public transportation, water, parks and recreation, and road maintenance all possess clearly defined roles. We all understand clearly what they do and don't expect them to be doing anything else. Unlike a police agency, the water department does not receive hundreds of phone calls a day for which someone might ask, "What in the world do we do with this one?"

Order Maintenance as the Police Mission

A significant part of the ambiguity surrounding the definition of police mission is the unfortunate use of the term "order maintenance" as synonymous with "conflict management." The so-called order maintenance function of the police is then held in contrast to the law enforcement function, i.e., order maintenance versus law enforcement. Characterized in this way, the two are co-equal but potentially conflicting police missions. Hence, we hear discussions that typically are as follows:

> It is symptomatic of our disproportionate identification with the crime control function that 90% of training is dedicated to law enforcement while 90% of the calls are order maintenance.

Order maintenance, modified by the word "temporal" is better viewed as the police mission, the *raison d'etre* of police organizations. Temporal order maintenance can be thought of as maintaining the status quo, i.e., keeping society stable and functioning by acceptable rules, by using interventions with short-term effects. Order maintenance used without the word "temporal" is too broad. Government itself maintains order. The police are responsible only for temporal, or short duration, issues.

Consistent with the concept of a hierarchy of organizational goals, we can then think of the mission of temporal order maintenance as subsuming at least three strategic objectives: public service/public safety, conflict management, and law enforcement. Illustrations of the types of calls for service that generally fall into each of these three categories are contained in Figure 4.1.

Figure 4.1 also illustrates two other important phenomena. First, different intervention techniques are preferred depending upon the on-scene objective The public service/public safety role is most often fulfilled by using social counseling. Comfort provided in delivering a death message, reassurance offered parents of a lost child and warnings to children and citizens to stay back from downed power wires all fall under the rubric of social counseling. Conflict management, however, demands a different response. Here authoritative persuasion is preferred. Police officers still aren't literally enforcing the law in this role, but they do employ their authority as a "law enforcement officer" to add strength to their persuasive talents. They do not, however, respond to these calls intending to arrest anyone. Finally, there is that category of responsibilities that is indeed law enforcement, and here the preferred intervention technique is arrest. The police do not respond to a robbery in progress with any intent to counsel or persuade, only to take someone into custody.

Figure 4.1

Police Objectives and Illustrative Problems

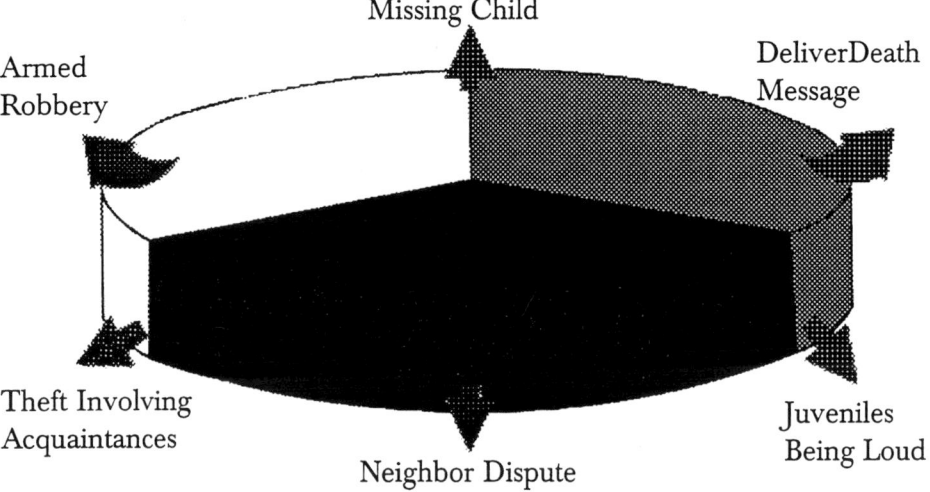

The second phenomenon illustrated by Figure 4.1 is the fact that both the on-scene objective of the police and their preferred intervention technique are best represented as a continuum of responses, not separate categories. Hence, a report of juveniles being loud is not clearly either public service/public safety or conflict management. Likewise, a theft involving acquaintances, or even an auto theft report, isn't always law enforcement—many times these turn out to be conflict management situations. Furthermore, a problem that initially is likely to be a public service/public safety issue, e.g., a report of a lost child, may occasionally turn out to be a law enforcement issue, e.g., kidnapping. Likewise, a report of loud juveniles may be a fight over a drug sale. Hence, the police respond to a given situation with an assumed on-scene objective and with a preferred intervention technique, but both may change rapidly with further information. Indeed, the behavior of respondents at a scene often changes the preferred police intervention technique. In a conflict management situation, a belligerent respondent may evoke an arrest intervention, despite the fact that the definition of the situation remains conflict management. Thus, a given on-scene objective may be achieved by various intervention techniques or combination of techniques. Clear, mutually exclusive, categorical objectives and intervention techniques do not exist. Instead a continuum of objectives and intervention techniques are intermingled, although patterns of association certainly are definable.

This makes sense if one recognizes that the overarching mission is temporal order maintenance. The police are at a scene fundamentally to maintain order, to keep the peace. As noted by Bittner (1990), "peacekeeping occasionally acquires the external aspects of law enforcement. This makes it specious to inquire whether or not police discretion in invoking the law conforms with the intention of some specific legal formula. The real reason behind an arrest is virtually always the actual state of particular social situations. . . ."

Peacekeeping, or temporal order maintenance, governs police response. But one must also not confuse law enforcement as an objective with arrest as a technique. It is such confusion that results in many scholars understating the importance of law enforcement as an element of policing. Law enforcement is not merely a technique. Arrest is a technique. Law enforcement is one of three primary strategic objectives subsumed by the mission of temporal order maintenance. There is a whole class of police activities focused exclusively upon this objective which have nothing to do with conflict management or public service/public safety.

This schematic also clarifies the issue of what constitutes "real" police work. Real police work is performing the role of a peace officer. Peacefulness, or orderliness, is the overall mission. A disorderly situation begets a call for police service or proactive police intrusion. Disorder ranges from downed power lines to robberies in progress.

There is, however, a hierarchical relationship among disorderly situations. As one moves from the public service/public safety class of situations through conflict management to law enforcement the threat to stable social order generally increases. Law enforcement situations usually result in greater harm and also possess the characteristic of being more generically threatening. Most public service/public safety and conflict management situations do not involve a general threat. Most also entail disorderly interactions among acquaintances (it may seem cold to think of delivering death messages in this way, but this task is essentially a "disorderly interaction among acquaintances." Because of the tendency for greater harm, and the more generic threat, the law enforcement role of the police predominates both resource allocation and public image. Nevertheless, it is but one element of keeping the peace.

Community-Oriented Policing

Sometimes form follows function, sometimes function follows form, and occasionally they interact. In the past ten years in policing, form and function have been interacting. Problem-oriented and community-oriented policing techniques have become alternate strategies to counseling, persuasion and arrest. Only by understanding this fact can one appreciate the depth of the current debate about these strategies. They are not merely a better way of doing things, they constitute doing different things.

Each strategy moves the police to a new role. The traditional mission has been temporal order maintenance. Both problem-oriented and community-oriented strategies may solve short-term problems, but they also push the police toward long-term structural and environmental interventions with significant community impact.

Community or problem-oriented techniques that are focused upon a very specific situation, in particular, repetitive calls for service from a single source, do not constitute a philosophical or mission switch. However, when the police begin to initiate the demolition of abandoned structures, supervise housing projects, or become involved in redrawing of zoning ordinances, a substantial change in mission has occurred. The police are no longer dealing with temporal order maintenance, but with long-term intervention in a community's infrastructure. The mission has changed from "temporal" order maintenance to "sustained" order maintenance. Police interventions are longer term and have a far more enduring impact. The three objectives of policing remain the same—public service/public safety, conflict management and law enforcement. The kinds of specific problems handled remain the same. But in addition to using social counseling, authoritative persuasion and arrest, the police employ social referral, extended counseling, or effect structural or environmental changes to provide a longer term, enduring impact. There is nothing wrong with such a change. But it is a significant one and should be approached carefully.

Further, community-oriented policing does not require abandoning current strategies. If the traditional model of policing has its faults, it also has its strengths. The pervasive bias in favor of entrepreneurial organizations in American culture can backfire on enterprises where innovation is either impossible, impractical, or simply not desirable. Elements of policing fit this criterion. In a headlong rush to prove to other police administrators that he or she is at the cutting edge, a police chief would do well to pause and consider the traditional police mission—temporal order maintenance, or stated differently, keeping things the way they are. Innovative, creative entrepreneurship doesn't always fit this mission. More frequently, staid, standardized, routinized bureaucratic response will best accomplish the goal of temporal order maintenance. The professional model may, in fact, be considerably better suited to fulfilling the mission of temporal order maintenance.

Analogies sometimes provide useful insight. Any analogy between policing and another enterprise has its limits, but one is particularly useful in understanding the match between police mission and police strategy. It is with the airline industry. Let's consider a flight from Chicago. The dynamics of a routine flight are these:

- The basic issue is to get to one's destination on schedule. Business meeting plans are made assuming a scheduled arrival. Regardless of all other considerations, the primary criterion is getting from point A to point B.
- Most people will bend by an hour or so on arrival time to stay on a particular airline if they are hooked on their frequent flyer program.
- Finally, most persons are reasonably tolerant of unavoidable delays. They irritate everyone, but 99.9% of the flying public

recognize that delays are an inevitable part of flying. The weather certainly can't be controlled, and equipment malfunctions can't be eliminated even with aggressive maintenance. Nevertheless, at the time a delay is announced most people are irritated.

It should be noted, however, that most people still don't enjoy flying. Probably the most salient issue of this respect is the cattle-herding phenomenon. Most recognize, however, that given the exigencies of flying that current technology will economically permit, there isn't anything any airline can do about it. The analogies with regard to policing are these:

- Despite analysis of calls for service indicating the predominance of conflict management calls, and despite the discussion in this chapter, the public regards the police role as crime control (just as the airlines' role is to get one from point A to point B). Police administrators would do well not to ignore this fact.
- The public appears willing to pay enough in taxes to get police services that exceed absolute minimums. There are some "no-frills" agencies, just as there are a few no-frills airlines. But the substantial majority of agencies are sufficiently funded to provide some training to their officers, some crime prevention effort, and an Explorer Scout program. Few communities, however, are willing to pay first-class fares, buying everything a police agency can possibly provide. Rather, most agencies feel some strain on resources.
- Many citizens will wait a while to talk to an officer they know rather than just any officer. Even these "frequent users," however, are unwilling to reschedule dramatically to stay with their favorite officer.
- Analogous to airline delays, the public recognizes that in the big picture the police can't solve every crime, can't resolve every problem. Nevertheless, they'll be irritated when it's their problem that can't be resolved. Further, they expect the police to make the best effort to solve their problem; and, at the least, to be courteous and honest in telling them that they can't.

It should be noted, however, that try as the police might, the substantial majority of the public will never "enjoy" contact with the police. Just as the airlines can't do anything about the herding phenomenon that makes air travel tedious, the police will always be associated with "trouble."

At the risk of stretching this analogy to the breaking point, it is also instructive to note what most expect of an airline once they show up to board a flight:

- An accessible reservations clerk
- A window or aisle seat
- Prompt departure
- Quick beverage service
- Luggage on the same flight
- The engine to stay bolted on
- Courteous staff (not gratuitous, not officious, not bubbly - just courteous)

In short, the public wants an efficient, competent–but very routine bureaucratic response. What they explicitly do not want is:

- Creative routing of luggage through Tokyo
- An innovative seat assignment
- Imaginative flying at non-prescribed altitudes
- Novel food (particularly when they have no menu choices)
- Inventive landing techniques

A significant portion of policing should meet the same criterion–an efficient, competent bureaucratic response–and nothing more. For example, a large part of the police function is simple information processing. These "take a report" calls, including minor traffic accidents, are best handled by highly routine, standardized procedures. Further, the best response to some types of calls is with a highly prescribed technique, e.g., delivering death messages or issuing traffic citations.

The problem is that a simple, efficient, prescribed bureaucratic response isn't inherently exciting to academics, research organizations, management consultants and change-oriented police managers. Indeed, there is a strong bias in the management literature in favor of entrepreneurial organizations. Advocates of bureaucratic efficiency in policing are now labeled "traditionalists," with all the negative connotations that the term implies.

But the reality is that classical bureaucratic efficiency is serving some organizations very well. Rensis Likert observed that Ray Kroc did not invent anything. The most successful food service enterprise the world has ever known was built, and continues to grow, on turn-of-the-century efficiency management principles. And whether one walks into a McDonalds in New York, Moscow, London or Tokyo, the service and product will always be the same—standardization taken to the extreme.

Similarly, the airline industry has prospered in the past twenty years, passenger miles increasing several times over, by doing the basics better. The relevance of such comparisons to policing is, of course, limited. Police agencies differ not only in the public versus private dimension, but numerous others as well. Nevertheless, we need to be cognizant of the fact that success does not always require daily creativity.

Yet, almost universally the traditional model of policing is disdained. Certainly, aspects of the model are either no longer necessary or no longer serving us as well as alternatives might. But not everything about the professional model should be discarded.

Herbert Simon (1945) argued in *Administrative Behavior* that efficiency is a completely neutral concept. It is neither inherently good nor bad. Mintzberg (1989) points out, however, that "A management obsessed with efficiency is a management obsessed with measurement. The cult of efficiency is the cult of calculation. And therein lies the problem." But too many police administrators and scholars throw out the baby with the bathwater. Obsession with superficial efficiency measures of elements of police operations does not require as a reaction eliminating the operations. There is a difference between overrating response time measures as a criterion of success and response time being meaningless.

Before we abandon the professional model we would do well to consider what it has bequeathed us. More educated and better trained personnel, sophisticated use of technology, better adherence to due process, far less corruption, and—yes—better response time are all the products of the Vollmer and Wilson legacy. Perhaps the legacy should not so readily be disdained because of some negative elements. Professional efficiency may not be such a bad idea.

The arguments presented here are not intended to imply that we reject the community-oriented model of policing. It is for some communities or even a large number of communities. But an evaluation can be made only after a clear definition has been established. A vague philosophy suggesting that we treat citizens responsively is a characteristic of any democratic model of policing, not just community-oriented policing.

Organizational Values

An organization without clearly defined, universally understood and accepted values is like a ship wandering aimlessly in a vast ocean. One must navigate the treacherous seas with a sense of direction and purpose. Without values, a police organization will accomplish nothing except maintaining the status quo. A mission statement alone will not do. If a police chief or sheriff has no vision and is in a strictly survival or "don't rock the boat" mode, lofty mission statements will mean nothing. If the leader isn't motivated, it is rare for others in that organization to be.

The first step in developing a sense of purpose is the establishment of a shared vision for the organization. This vision should be developed by the police chief or sheriff. It sets the course by providing an articulated point of view to guide organizational personnel. The vision must include a guideline for its achievement.

The second step is the development by all stakeholders (i.e., police department members, city/county officials and the community) of a clear and concise statement of the organization's mission or purpose. All stakeholders should have input, but clearly it should be based on the vision set by the chief or sheriff. It provides the foundation upon which all operational decisions and organizational directives are based. The Bloomingdale, Illinois Police Department's mission is: "The Mission for every member of the department is to consistently seek and find ways to affirmatively promote, preserve and deliver a feeling of security, safety and quality services to members of our community." This mission statement is not only posted throughout the police department, but it is reinforced by having every police department employee annually sign acceptance of this mission, as well as the Code of Ethics and Oath of Office. Further, the mission statement is referenced in every performance evaluation, and every recording of positive or negative discipline.

A trainer in communication and team building routinely asks his audience of police employees if each department represented has a written department mission. About 25 percent respond that they don't, 25 percent respond that they're not sure, and 50 percent respond, quite proudly, that they do. He then takes out a $20 bill, throws it on the table, and offers it to anyone in the room who can recite one or two consecutive sentences of their mission statement. Never has he had to pay out the $20! A mission statement buried in a binder, gathering dust on the shelf is useless. It certainly isn't being operationalized.

The third step is establishing the organization's values. Values are the beliefs that guide an organization and the behavior of its employees. The same stakeholders should identify the primary values of the organization and develop clear and concise value statements based on the vision. This set of values should reflect beliefs, be truthful, doable and real, and should be clearly articulated to the department and community. There should be both an organizational and individual commitment to these values as the basis for making decisions. They are a guide in exercising discretion. The Elgin, Illinois Police Department, for example, established the following values categories for their organization:

1. Human Life
2. Integrity
3. Laws and Constitution
4. Excellence
5. Accountability
6. Cooperation
7. Problem-solving
8. Ourselves

A value statement for problem-solving is, "We are most effective when we help identify and solve community problems;" for integrity, "We believe integrity is the basis for community trust." Values must be institutionalized and may very well require changing the culture of the organization. Institutionalizing of values should occur in recruitment, selection, training, supervision, policy statements, leadership, rewards, sanctions, media relations, and certainly in departmental management.

The last step in defining and promoting values is the setting and prioritization of goals of the organization. Clear and concise goal statements are based on the vision.

Codes of Ethics

In developing an organizational ethic, one must understand that ethics programs are not substitutes for the real thing. Turning ethics into a buzzword or an organizational program will not guarantee integrity in an organization. Employees have a built-in "genius" for discovering the real reason for a program and learn quickly how to satisfy its minimum requirements. The best way to develop an organizational ethic is the simplest way. If the CEO truly believes that honesty and respect for others are priorities, employees will follow the lead.

Most police departments adopt the code of ethics that is published by the International Association of Chiefs of Police. However, few officers are familiar with the code. As with any profession, there is an informal code of ethics prevalent through the work environment. Generally, this code stipulates right from wrong. Occasionally conduct with which the chief or sheriff may be uncomfortable is acceptable within the informal code of ethics. A frequent example is acceptance of gratuities. Almost universally, police departments prohibit the acceptance of gifts, gratuities, bribes, or rewards. Tradition and individual values often create a conflict, and it is not uncommon to find that officers routinely accept minor gifts, such as coffee, reduced rates for services, etc. In exceptional cases, such as the holidays, a department may consider accepting food gift baskets, if they are made available to all employees. Gifts which violate departmental policy should be returned with a letter explaining the policy. The CEO must be an example of the agency's gratuity policy!

Work Ethic

Subordinates tend to look to the work ethic of the "boss" to determine what the acceptable work ethic is for the organization. Little things, like the time the chief reports for work and the time he/she leaves, sets an unofficial standard and becomes an organizational benchmark. A police chief or sheriff should not expect to receive praise from subordinates or elected officials about her/his positive work ethic. It is part of one's responsibility in the CEO role, and is simply expected.

Chapter 5

MANAGING THE AGENCY'S CRITICAL COMPONENTS

Human Resource Issues

SUCCESSFUL MANAGEMENT DEMANDS THAT POLICE EXECUTIVES integrate critical agency policy and operations with mission, values, and infrastructure. Agency management is not neatly conceptualized into distinct categories. A mission statement only becomes meaningful when it is operationalized into programming. Programming success requires leadership. Leadership requires a clear understanding of the role of management. This chapter reviews several critical components of successful management: human resource issues, legal liability, technology integration and critical incident planning. Without appropriate systems in place to assure reasonably smooth operations, investment in leadership and mission planning is for naught.

Human resource planning includes recruitment, training, development, evaluation, and discipline of personnel. As executives across the nation know, the quality of personnel and their management is the most important factor that affects the services provided by the organization. It is therefore imperative that the human resource policies of a police organization support the objectives of that agency.

Recruiting and Hiring

The person hired today for a law enforcement agency position, either sworn or civilian, will impact the direction of that agency for years to come. That employee will probably remain with the department for twenty or more years, and will reflect the professionalism and ethical behavior of the department during that time. The type of personnel hired under a chief or sheriff communicates to the community the philosophy and leadership style of the chief executive.

Although it is important that employees reflect the attitude, demeanor, and professional bearing of the chief, and hence the agency, it is also important that the department's composition reflect the make-up of the community. The community's education, race/ethnicity, gender, and perhaps even religious diversity should be represented by agency personnel. Some departments have been ordered by a court or federal agency to employ personnel that reflect the make-up of the community. Not only is it demeaning for a department to be regulated by outside agencies, such regulation may affect department morale. The chief should oversee the recruiting and hiring processes to ensure that the people preferred by the agency are in fact recruited and hired.

To target citizens that are desirable employees, the police department has to actively recruit. Unfortunately, in the past many law enforcement agencies did not recruit–they just selected from among those who applied (Moore & Stephens, 1991). With the advent of affirmative action and the need for qualified personnel, a more proactive method of recruitment is needed. Advertisements in targeted newspapers and other media; direct recruitment at community colleges and universities; networking with civic and community leaders; and other proactive efforts should result in an applicant pool that is qualified and reflective of the community. Another recruitment activity that should not be ignored is attendance at high school career days. This activity may not pay-off for several years, however, early exposure to law enforcement as a career may have a pronounced impact.

The chief must not forget that current personnel are the best recruiters for the department. Not only do employees recruit directly, but they are ambassadors of the agency in every encounter with the public. If the public's perception of the agency is one of bias toward and unfair treatment of minorities it becomes very difficult to recruit minority persons. It is, therefore, imperative that the daily actions of officers reflect the mission and goals of the department. Recruitment efforts are profoundly affected by the agency's reputation, standing in the community and daily encounters between employees and the public.

Following recruitment, the selection procedure begins. There are two theories concerning selection. The first is to select the right type of person regardless of the position. The second theory proposes selecting applicants who already possess the skills, knowledge, abilities, and other characteristics needed for the job as determined by a job task analysis (Sheehan and Cordner, 1995). The first is accomplished by hiring those applicants who are the most mature, intelligent, and stable, then training them for the position. According to Sheehan and Cordner (1995), the second theory emphasizes mechanical and quantifiable aspects of the job rather than people skills. Some agencies focus exclusively on one theory in their selection process while other agencies select based on some combination of the two.

Depending upon governmental structure, an agency may utilize a police and fire commission, a civil service commission, the city/county personnel department or its own personnel unit to conduct the selection procedures. Whatever division is involved in choosing and implementing the selection procedures, the chief and that unit must ensure the procedures are fair and job related.

After recruiting and selecting the most qualified candidates, newly hired employees must be trained in state mandated courses, as well as the department's policies and procedures. After completion of the state mandated basic recruit training program, many agencies have the newly hired officer complete a department field training program. If the agency has such a program, the chief should ensure that the program reflects the agency mission and values and that those elements are included in the evaluation of the trainees.

PERSONNEL TRAINING AND CAREER DEVELOPMENT. Law enforcement is constantly changing. As personnel practices, technology, and demands for police services change and criminals become more sophisticated, traditional police practices are questioned. Change and reform have become imperative. Law enforcement executives must be prepared to meet the changing needs of the workforce and of society. One way to meet these demands is to develop an education, training, and professional development strategy that will serve the community and the agency.

In-service training can increase professionalism, enhance officer and citizen safety and directly and indirectly reduce liability. This is an integral component of the training strategy the chief institutes. In-service training can update all employees of changes in laws, procedures, and policies; and can include state mandated courses. It is also an opportunity to train personnel in specific areas where deficiencies may exist, as identified by a training needs assessment. Such areas may include report writing, communication skills, handling mentally disturbed individuals or pursuit driving. Finally, in-service training can provide training that incorporates the mission and values established by the chief.

Professional development should be encouraged for all employees. Only twenty percent of all employees will become supervisors and managers. It is important to provide new challenges and job enrichment for those who choose to remain at the level of operations or who are unable to be promoted. As more and more tasks are being demanded of the patrol officer, professional development is needed to develop the skills needed in this expanded role and for officers to increase responsibility and develop greater autonomy (Moore and Stephens, 1991). The chief or sheriff must be committed to this strategy to ensure that resources are available for employee participation in technical, specialized, and management training. A career development program will help retain motivated, self-starting employees and will reward them for developing skills essential to their role in the agency. However, professional development must not only enrich the individual, it must also fulfill a need that the agency is experiencing. All decisions concerning professional development must, therefore, fit a two-prong test: (1) will the program meet a need or deficiency in the department, and (2) will it meet the goals of the individual?

To encourage professional development of employees, the chief might develop a scheme in which each employee is rewarded for the skills that he/she possesses as well as the seniority and rank upon which salary and benefits are commonly based. This may take some refinement and several years, as often pay scales and benefits are dictated by the contract between the officers' union and the jurisdiction. Chiefs will need to show the benefits that the program has to individual employees, the department, and the community to obtain support for this program.

A problem faced by sheriffs, and police chiefs who operate lock-ups, is how to develop the corrections officer position as an end onto itself. In most counties, the corrections officer is seen as a stepping stone to becoming a deputy sheriff. When this happens the jail is continuously recruiting, hiring, and training new employees, a costly undertaking. To retain corrections officers and to encourage employees to remain in the jail, a career ladder within that area should be created.

Promoting employees to specialist positions or supervisory/management roles can be rewarding, yet can create problems for the chief. The chief wants to promote those employees who have shown support for the chief's vision, mission, and values, yet any promotion process must be fair and based on the established promotion procedure. Promotion screening may include written tests, oral boards, and/or assessment centers, and take into account candidate training, education, experience and supervisor recommendations. To be fair, positions must be posted and list the required qualifications and process.

PERFORMANCE EVALUATIONS. Employee performance evaluation has been used in law enforcement agencies for years and has become a basic element of effective public organizations. The performance evaluation can provide feedback to the employee concerning work behavior and objectives to be met; furnish information to management for staffing, directing and controlling decisions; create a record to be used for promotion purposes; and provide guidance of what is important to achieve (Moore & Stephens, 1991; Sheehan & Cordner, 1995). Unfortunately, there are few organizations that are satisfied with their performance evaluation program. Most are constantly searching for a better method.

Evaluations can take many forms. At one end of the spectrum is a blank sheet of paper considered by many managers to be the best form. This model has supervisors write a narrative of the positive and negative performances of the employee. At the other extreme is a printed form with weighted ratings of selected traits and tasks that are appropriate for the position. In this model, supervisors check the appropriate box for each trait or job task being evaluated, then scores are added to determine the employee's effectiveness. In some cases employees are ranked with others who perform the same role.

Performance evaluations can be based on counting activities, such as number of arrests, sick days taken, traffic citations issued and number of convictions. Other performance evaluations measure job activities such as citizen satisfaction with officer response and officer judgment. The quantitative evaluations are seen as being impartial and relatively easy to determine. However, they have several disadvantages such as oversimplifying the job and overlooking important tasks or activities that are not easily counted. Too often performance measures evaluate one aspect of the job and are not necessarily an indicator of overall job performance (Froemel, 1979). On the other hand, while measuring traits and skills such as customer satisfaction and judgment can reflect the activities of the officer more accurately, they are more susceptible to error and can be more open to question and challenge. Some agencies find it best to combine the two methods.

The trend in law enforcement performance evaluations is to utilize the key components of the written job description and to assess a simple "competent" or "needs improvement" for each essential task. In this manner, the evaluation focuses on the quality of the work and not on personality issues (Jones, 1998). This also allows the evaluation process to be more objective and keeps the focus on tasks that are to be performed by the worker and that are tangible and readily observed. Supervisors should be encouraged to maintain written performance logs that give specific examples of both good and poor evaluation. A short narrative regarding the development goals that have been agreed upon by the rater and the employee should also be included in this evaluation form. Finally, the evaluator should identify employees' skills that can be capitalized upon and those skills that are weak and need improvement. Whichever type of evaluation is used, it requires someone, preferably the chief executive, to make decisions concerning what is important so that those tasks and skills are evaluated.

Unfortunately, the performance evaluation process can be political. Job evaluations can never be totally objective. Organization politics will always play a role. Some political actions involved in the performance evaluation process include deliberate manipulation of formal ratings, which could occur if the evaluators' job performance is based in part on his/her subordinates evaluations. Other political actions that could take place during evaluations is a lower rating that is used to show the subordinate who is boss or to shock the subordinate into increasing performance. Those being evaluated can also manipulate the system by engaging in favorable behavior close to evaluation time.

In the "ideal world," performance evaluations should be linked to compensation increases or merit pay. Civil service systems and unions resist this linkage and usually strive to have a collective bargaining agreement that ignores performance and bases pay increases solely upon longevity.

The chief executive may want to consider adopting both an informal progress review as well as the more formal performance evaluation. The informal review allows the supervisor and the employee to examine the employee's progress on a regular basis. This allows goals and objectives to be adjusted, if needed, and allows the supervisor to correct any errors that the employee may be making (Universal Training Systems Company, 1976).

The formal evaluation process is a written analysis of past performance during the time span of the review, including performance on regular tasks and special projects, establishing new goals, and planning career development. This evaluation usually becomes part of the employee personnel file and is used during the next evaluation to assess if the established objectives and goals have been met.

Regardless of the evaluation format, the evaluation is a "subjective" process that is difficult to prepare, explain, and justify. Ironically, very few performance evaluations, with the exception of the extreme "poor performance," are negative. The natural aversion to conflict by most supervisors results in "routine evaluations" with little feedback to the employee regarding future development needs. In actuality, that is exactly what an effective performance evaluation should focus upon—what behavior, conduct, and skills should be changed and/or developed. No matter what format is used, the employee evaluation can be an uncomfortable experience. To eliminate or at least decrease these feelings, the performance evaluation process must include training of both evaluators and those being evaluated. This will allow all parties involved to review the process to be used and become knowledgeable about its purposes. Evaluators are familiarized with the rating system and the completion of the evaluation. Training should also teach evaluators how to provide both positive and negative feedback and to provide assistance in both skill improvement and career development.

A performance evaluation appeal process is essential to resolve disagreements that occur between the rater and the employee that cannot be resolved in a performance evaluation interview. A procedure should be in place outlining the appeal process and what limits exist to make change. Performance evaluations can be open to legal action, especially if the evaluation is used to make employment decisions, such as termination, pay increases or promotion. Employees can contest the content of the evaluation as well as the reliability and validity of the process. It is, therefore, important to ensure that the performance evaluation process is job-related, based on the duties and responsibilities for the position being evaluated and is derived from a job analysis or up-to-date job description. The process must also be documented, the supervisor must record facts on important incidents. The chief executive must also ensure that the performance evaluation does not create unnecessary adverse impact and is defensible if challenged.

Even though the performance evaluation can be fraught with problems, the chief executive can ensure that the goal of the evaluation process is achieved if policies and procedures are established and followed, and the performance standards are reasonable, attainable, and relevant (Jones, 1998). To have a successful performance evaluation process, periodic evaluations of the system must be done, including getting input from the raters and those being rated concerning the form, what is evaluated, the method of evaluation, and other elements of the process. Additionally, management must practice what it preaches. Managers and supervisors should be evaluated by their superiors using the same process that is in effect for other employees (Bopp & Whisenand, 1980). Whatever system is used, it should be simple, linked to tasks, skills, and knowledge needed for the job; possess clearly defined job aspects to be evaluated, identify the scale or system used to rate the job tasks and characteristics, keep the paperwork to a minimum, and include training on the performance evaluation process.

Civil Liability of Law Enforcement Executives

A sportswriter once wrote, "There were two types of professional football coaches: those that have been fired and those that are going to be fired." A variant of this somewhat cynical observation may be applied to police chiefs and sheriffs. The two types of law enforcement executives are those that have been sued and those that are going to be sued. The level of hierarchical responsibility, the high public profile, the oversight of potentially risky activities, an increasingly litigious society and a civil justice system with a focus on individual rights rather than societal responsibilities place the modern law enforcement executive squarely in the path of litigation. Additionally, certain factors in the operation of the civil justice system—such as the possibility of lucrative attorney's fees being awarded even in weak cases—add to the potential for suit. Certainly, examples may be found of police executives who have completed a career without ever having sat on the wrong side of the courtroom. However, such examples are becoming increasingly rare.

As a chief of police or sheriff, the senior law enforcement executive obviously occupies the top position in the agency's hierarchy. Individuals who believe they have been wronged by an employee of the agency normally assume that the agency head bears responsibility. This perspective exists whether the alleged wrong was at the hands of a deputy sheriff in a five-member department or a patrol officer in a large city such as Chicago. The public assumes the chief executive must be held responsible. While this notion may be politically appropriate, it is frequently incorrect legally. Public accountability and legal liability are not congruent concepts. History is riddled with tales of individuals who were turned out of office based on the unacceptable behavior of their subordinates. The same individuals were found not liable for monetary damages in those incidents.

A sheriff or chief of police must maintain a high public profile. The nature of the job requires frequent interaction with all segments of the public. This translates into appearing on radio and television and in the print media, giving speeches at community association meetings, and, in the case of a sheriff, actually touting one's talents to the public during an election. There is constant name reinforcement to the general public. Thus, when a lawsuit is contemplated against a community's law enforcement agency, the agency head, whose name is often synonymous with the agency, is named in the suit. Consider the city public works department. When a sanitary sewer line backs up and floods a citizen's home, the city may be sued. Is the public works department head also named? When a municipal refuse truck sideswipes a resident's vehicle, is the department head named in the lawsuit? Most often the answer is, of course, no.

By its very nature, the law enforcement function involves high-risk activities. Most employees carry instruments of deadly force. Encounters with citizens are often emotionally charged. Penal law enforcement responsibilities require the exercise of discretion on the part of individual officers. County correctional operations are responsible for food, shelter, clothing, health, and safety of prisoners. These are only a few examples of police activities that, if not performed appropriately, can give rise to unhappy citizens and civil lawsuits. Even the sheer number of miles logged in police vehicles increases the potential for "fender benders" and corresponding civil liability.

Much has been written about our so-called litigious society. A generation ago, lawsuits were viewed as a last resort to resolving a personal dispute. Today, the number of lawsuits filed has expanded exponentially. In U.S. District Court alone, over 250,000 civil suits were filed in 1997. The number of pending civil cases in state trial courts now exceeds 14 million! Clogged court dockets have in many communities greatly slowed the wheels of criminal and civil justice. While certainly only a small fraction of these suits are against law enforcement personnel, there is little reason to believe that the number of such lawsuits has not also increased proportionally over the last quarter century. Some argue that the increased volume of litigation is directly related to the number of lawyers in society. Certainly, a finite number of attorneys can only handle a finite number of claims; increase the number of lawyers and, correspondingly, the number of lawsuits can be expected to increase—young lawyers also have to eat. In 1996, the Bureau of Labor Statistics reported over 600,000 practicing lawyers in America.

The very nature of American society is grounded in the concept of individual rights and liberties. These individual rights and liberties, most derived from the U.S. Constitution, often conflict with society's efforts to maintain public order through the law enforcement function. An individual who believes his rowdy behavior is merely an exercise of his free speech right will likely be unhappy to be arrested for disorderly conduct—a potential false arrest suit. Even an uncooperative intoxicated driver may view the police use of force to subdue him as excessive and warranting a civil claim. (Consider the infamous *Rodney King* case in Los Angeles in this regard.) Conversely, many freedom-loving Americans hold the view that government has a responsibility to protect its citizenry. Thus, when the police response to a 911 call is misdispatched or slow-arriving and a citizen is raped, injured, or killed, litigation against the governmental agency may follow.

Without doubt, one of the primary factors spurring civil litigation against law enforcement agencies is the partial abrogation of the doctrine of sovereign immunity. For many years, most states followed the common law doctrine of sovereign immunity in regard to civil suits against governmental entities and their officials and employees. Simply stated, this doctrine holds that a sovereign cannot be sued without its permission, and traditionally permission was rarely forthcoming. Consequently, citizens who were harmed by official misconduct had little recourse. About 50 years ago, the federal government and the states began loosening their adherence to the rule, first in breach of contract cases and later in personal injury matters.

Today, traditional tort suits against state and local governmental entities are regulated by state statutes. For example, Illinois governmental entities and officials are controlled by the Local Governmental and Governmental Employees Tort Immunity Act, 745 ILCS 10/. For violations of constitutionally protected rights, the United States Supreme Court ruled in 1978 that the doctrine of sovereign immunity was unavailable as a defense and local governmental units could, under certain conditions, be held civilly liable. This ruling, in Monell v. New York City Department of Social Services, 436 U.S. 658 (1978), is believed by many legal scholars to have substantially facilitated civil litigation in the law enforcement field.

The decision allows an aggrieved plaintiff to not only pursue a cause of action against the offending police officer or police official but, more importantly, against the "deep pockets" of the employing municipality. This latter aspect has the secondary effect of actually reducing the likelihood that a police official, as an individual, will be forced to pay any monetary judgment that might be awarded. Since a city or county has the power to tax, its fiscal resources can be viewed as virtually limitless. In contrast, the individual net worth of police chiefs, sheriffs and other peace officers is rarely great. The goal of the plaintiff's attorney then is to establish liability on the part of the party with the resources to pay a judgment–the governmental entity. An uncollectable monetary award against a chief of police or sheriff is of little use to an injured citizen or her/his lawyer.

Finally, most state and federal fair employment laws have been extended to public employers in recent years. Thus, a police chief or sheriff may be subject to suit for alleged unlawful discrimination in making employment decisions or for failure to properly compensate employees for overtime. For a variety of reasons that will be explored subsequently, suits by employees are increasingly more likely than suits by the public at large.

CATEGORIES OF SUITS. Lawsuits against public officials have their origins in one of three legal theories:

1. Common law tort
2. Constitutional tort
3. Federal and state labor and personnel statutes

A tort is defined as a civil wrong in which the action of one person causes injury to the person or property of another, in violation of a legal duty imposed by law. Lawsuits arising from automobile collisions, injuries from defective products and harm due to another person's negligence are examples of torts found in everyday life. The law enforcement professional faces legal exposure in tort for conduct resulting from claims of assault and battery, false arrest, false imprisonment, and wrongful death. Of particular concern to administrators are suits arising from patrol vehicle collisions during pursuits and a myriad of injuries that can occur in a jail.

As noted earlier, for many years governmental units and their employees were protected from such claims under the doctrine of sovereign immunity. This protection is eroding. For example, some years ago the Illinois legislature waived immunity for selected torts, thereby permitting some claims to be pursued against governmental units. Under the Local Governmental and Governmental Employees Tort Immunity Act, however, public officials and employees still enjoy a high degree of immunity. Specifically, immunity is retained for injuries arising out of policy decisions or the exercise of discretion. Likewise, there is a granting of immunity for employees who are acting within the scope of their employment. Finally, law enforcement personnel are also immune from liability for injuries arising out of the provision of police services and certain aspects of jail operations. The statute further requires provision of legal defense and indemnity to public employees subject to tort claims. Indemnity is not permitted for punitive damages. Most other states have similar statutes.

Because of the barriers created by the doctrine of sovereign immunity and state statutes, plaintiffs' attorneys often make their claims under the guise of a so-called constitutional tort. These are claims based on allegations of violations of constitutional rights under a federal statute, Title 42 U.S. Code § 1983. Commonly referred to as "1983 suits," these actions are often pursued in federal court. False arrest, use of force and illegal search suits are based on allegations of violation of the Fourth Amendment protection against unreasonable searches and seizures while prisoner suits often arise from Eighth Amendment claims, being subjected to cruel and unusual punishment. Law enforcement employees sue their employers often under a claim of a First Amendment free speech violation, or when adverse personnel action is taken, an alleged deprivation of due process under the Fourteenth Amendment.

For the law enforcement administrator to have personal liability, the plaintiff must show that the administrator either intentionally deprived him or her of a constitutional right or was "deliberately indifferent," resulting in the right being violated. Because of Supreme Court decisions in recent years, the deliberate indifference standard has become increasingly difficult for a plaintiff to establish. Essentially, an aggrieved party must show that the police official made a conscious choice to ignore a constitutional right, mere negligent behavior is insufficient. A variety of other legal defenses may also be available to the official.

While a police official may escape personal liability, the employing agency may be held legally responsible if the unconstitutional act was a policy or custom of the agency. Thus, for example, a use of force policy later found to be unconstitutional may result in legal liability for a municipality while police officers who acted under the policy escape responsibility. This is exactly what occurred when the Supreme Court declared the common law fleeing felon rule unconstitutional in Tennessee v. Garner, 471 U.S. 1 (1985). The city of Memphis was found civilly liable because its policy of using deadly force against any fleeing felon violated the Fourth Amendment. However, the police officer who fired the fatal shot into the back of 15-year-old Edward Garner was excused from civil responsibility.

This individual/agency liability distinction poses a particular problem for law enforcement administrators. Since a city or county makes its policies through the decisions of its elected and appointed officials, a judgment that a police leader makes can place the employing entity in danger of civil liability. For the actions of a police chief or sheriff to constitute "policy" of the city or county, the police chief or sheriff must be legally considered a "policymaker." This status may vary depending upon the topic in question. For example, the average police chief could be considered a "policymaker" regarding personnel shift assignments because that action is normally not subject to review by higher authorities. On the other hand, the same chief might not be a "policymaker" in employee discipline if a city manager, mayor or other official originally approved the disciplinary procedure. Thus, under Section 1983, a law enforcement official's decision, which later proved unconstitutional, could expose a municipality or county to monetary liability, while at the same time the official would not have corresponding personal liability. The complexities of 1983 suits mandate that public officials engage competent legal counsel to determine their personal legal exposure.

The third area of possible personal liability exposure arises from federal and state fair employment and labor laws. Subordinate employees or employee unions are almost always the plaintiffs in such cases. Most often the suits do not actually expose the agency administrator to personal liability. Rather, the aggrieved employee is seeking relief that can be granted only by the agency, e.g., promotion, back pay, overtime compensation. A few statutes do provide for suits against individuals. Sexual harassment claims come most readily to mind. Other adverse personnel actions brought against a sheriff or police chief normally are constitutionally based and pursued as a 1983 suit.

Suits originating in fair employment and labor law violations rarely come as a surprise. In virtually all instances, exhaustion of administrative remedies is a prerequisite to the filing of the suit. Thus, the agency head will have either already reviewed the claim or have been a participant in a hearing before a merit board, a hearing officer or an arbitrator.

A LAWSUIT DOES NOT MEAN LIABILITY. A basic, but often misunderstood point, is that the filing of a lawsuit does not mean that the defendant has any legal liability. It does not even say much about the likelihood of success on the part of the plaintiff. Unlike the filing of criminal charges where a state's attorney, a grand jury or a judge makes a determination of probable cause before charges are formally pressed, no similar requirement exists in the civil side of the courthouse. All that is required to file a civil lawsuit is payment of a filing fee and a verification by the plaintiff's lawyer that the petition's allegation is "well grounded in fact and is warranted by existing law." Curiously, only in the most extreme cases (e.g., repetitive filing of truly frivolous lawsuits) is a sanction imposed for making allegations that are subsequently shown not to be true.

This lack of litigation screening not only fills courts with arguably weak claims but also places a law enforcement official in a quandary. Assume, for example, that an officer arrests an individual for shoplifting. In the course of processing the suspect, the arresting officer finds stolen merchandise in her purse. The individual, the wife of a local bank president, nevertheless denies the charges. At trial, the judge dismisses the case on the grounds that the search of the purse was unconstitutional. The defendant goes free. In an effort to regain her reputation and to express her unhappiness with the police, she sues the officer, the chief of police and the municipality. She alleges that she was treated rudely, had excessive force used against her, was falsely arrested and searched, and otherwise had her constitutional rights violated. If the matter ever goes to trial, the facts may clearly establish that the allegations are not substantiated, that the officer acted lawfully and that none of the parties are civilly liable. Nevertheless, when the suit is filed, the local media may widely report the matter. Normally, when such matters are reported, the agency head is asked for a comment. Because the chief may be unaware of the details of the case or because the municipality's attorney may caution against public comment on pending litigation, the police executive may be forced to make no comment. All that the public knows is the allegations and the lack of denial by the police department. If the matter is not formally resolved through trial or dismissal, the public is never informed of the correctness of the officer's conduct. For the law enforcement executive, keeping an appropriate perspective about civil suits is vitally important.

LAWSUIT AS A WAKE-UP CALL. Even if a lawsuit is without legal merit, it is evidence that some citizen is unhappy with the actions of the law enforcement agency. A chief of police or sheriff should examine a lawsuit in the same manner that lesser complaints are reviewed. Most agencies have mechanisms for responding to citizen complaints. Minor complaints, such as officer discourtesy, may be reviewed by first line supervisors. More serious matters, such as excessive use of force, may warrant a formal internal affairs investigation. Allegations in lawsuits are no different. Whether or not civil liability is ultimately established, the suit should serve as an impetus for reviewing policies, field procedures, training, human resource practices, or other aspects of managing the department. Even a frivolous suit is proof that someone believes the agency has a problem. Corrective action may be necessary to head off later, more valid litigation. Changing a condition or procedure after harm has occurred is generally not admissible in court as proof that the original condition was improper.

EXECUTIVE IS OFTEN NECESSARY BUT MINOR PARTY. For a decade, George J. Beto served as Director of the Texas Department of Corrections, one of the nation's largest prison systems. Beto, who previously had been a member of the Illinois Parole and Pardons Board while employed as president of Concordia Theological Seminary in Springfield, by most historical accounts was well respected by inmates and prison employees alike. Yet, during his tenure as a prison administrator he held the dubious distinction of being the most sued man in America! Why? Simply because he was the boss. Few of the hundreds of suits were efforts to obtain a monetary judgment against Beto personally. Rather, as the director, he was a necessary defendant in any inmate's habeas corpus action or any suit contesting conditions of confinement. When he stepped down in 1972, his successor's name, W. J. Estelle, replaced him as the named defendant in the pending lawsuits.

Law enforcement executives are often named in suits in their "official capacity" because they are the boss. Plaintiffs' lawyers frequently take a shotgun approach and name as defendants every person in the chain of command of the offending officer. Thus, if a patrol officer is claimed to have violated a citizen's rights, the citizen might sue by name the officer, his sergeant, his lieutenant, his captain, the deputy chief, the chief of police, the department, and the municipality. Courts view a suit against a governmental official in his or her "official capacity" as simply a suit against the governmental employer, i.e., the city or county. The same is true regarding a suit against the "police department" or "sheriff's department." These divisions have no existence separate from the city or county government of which they are a part.

Unfortunately, circumstances do occur where the law enforcement executive is sued not only in "official capacity" but also in "individual capacity," or both. Individual capacity suits seek to hold the executive personally liable for the alleged harm. Sheriffs, because of being elected officials with a fair degree of autonomy from the remainder of county government, have greater exposure than police chiefs in this regard. The good news is that except for egregious intentional misconduct, e.g., torturing a prisoner, many jurisdictions will pay the legal representation bills of the official and indemnify the official in case of a monetary judgment. These costs are often covered by public official liability insurance.

EXECUTIVE HAS SEVERAL LEGAL DEFENSES AVAILABLE. When any civil suit is defended, two possible defenses automatically arise. First, a defendant will be found not liable if the plaintiff fails to establish a legally recognized cause of action. Courts entertain lawsuits only for harms that the law traditionally recognizes as actionable. For example, one of the more common forms of litigation is based on negligence arising out of an automobile collision. The law recognizes that a motorist has a duty to operate his automobile in a safe manner and if that motorist negligently causes personal injury or property damage to another, the courts will provide a forum to litigate the extent of liability. In contrast, if one individual behaves rudely toward another person, that rude behavior does not provide a basis for a civil suit; the law simply does not recognize a cause of action for rude behavior. For the public official, certain actions are simply not subject to civil court remedy. For instance, save for a few unusual cases, American courts have not allowed a disgruntled public employee to sue his employer because he was transferred to another assignment, even if he perceives the assignment to have less prestige. Thus, transferring a deputy sheriff from assignment as a detective to working in the county correctional facility will normally not be actionable so long as his compensation is not altered.

Besides the failure to state a cause of action, civil suits may also be defended on a factual basis. Simply put, the plaintiff might have a legitimate claim, but only if the facts were as alleged. For example, false imprisonment is certainly a long-recognized tort. But if the facts of the case establish that no deprivation of liberty occurred, or that the imprisonment was based on a valid court order and thus not false, the suit will fail.

Public officials, such as police chiefs and sheriffs, also enjoy some special defenses that can eliminate personal liability. (Bear in mind that these defenses may absolve the law enforcement executive from personal liability but the employing governmental agency may still be responsible.) At the forefront of defenses is the doctrine of qualified immunity. This doctrine is based upon the principle that public officials are employed to exercise their best judgment in performing their offices. Thus, if the law were to hold an official responsible for harm as a result of a discretionary decision, no one would want to be a public official. This doctrine holds true even when bad results occur. Consequently, a chief of police or sheriff is immune from civil suit for the results of a discretionary decision made within the scope of his or her employment. This defense is particularly appropriate in cases involving tactical or operational decisions.

For purposes of Section 1983 suits, the Supreme Court has ruled that a public official may be held liable only where the official knew or should have known that his or her actions were unconstitutional. In other words, to be liable for violating an individual's constitutional rights, the right must have been "clearly established" at the time of the infringement and it must be shown that the average law enforcement official would have known that the conduct was unconstitutional. For example, a sheriff who refuses to permit prisoners to use tobacco is likely not civilly liable for that decision even if a federal judge were to later rule that tobacco use while incarcerated is constitutionally protected. The reason: the law on tobacco use by prisoners is not clearly established because of the lack of definitive court decisions. The sheriff cannot be expected to guess what the law will ultimately turn out to be! In contrast, a sheriff who refuses a prisoner the opportunity to visit with his lawyer is on dangerous ground. The constitutional right to confer with legal counsel in preparation for trial is clearly established and the average sheriff knows, or should know, this principle.

Finally, the mere fact that a subordinate officer unlawfully injured an individual or his property does not automatically mean the agency head is responsible. The doctrine of *respondeat superior*—the master is responsible for the servant—is limited in its application in public sector cases. Specifically, the "master" is normally considered to be the employing entity, such as the city, not the agency head. Second, the agency head, like any other supervisor, is civilly liable only if he/she ordered, approved, directed, or was deliberately indifferent to the unlawful behavior. Unlike the ancient code of the sea where the ship's captain is totally responsible for what occurs under his command, the chief of police has no such absolute legal responsibility—and concurrent personal liability—for every action of a subordinate officer.

SUITS BY EMPLOYEES. Despite the attention given to civil liability for police misconduct, increasingly police administrators find themselves being sued, not by members of the public at large, but by subordinate employees! Personnel actions ranging from allegations of sex discrimination to denial of collective bargaining rights have burgeoned in the last 20 years. Several reasons exist for this phenomenon. First, in the overwhelming number of encounters with the public the police simply do not engage in misconduct. Second, the bulk of individuals who come into contact with the police on a regular basis would not be particularly sympathetic plaintiffs in a courtroom. Few lawyers can earn a living suing the police for conducting an illegal search that produces 200 pounds of cocaine. The average juror is unlikely to be sympathetic to the aggrieved drug dealer. Third, much police misconduct is handled internally to the satisfaction of the unhappy citizen. A citizen who is treated roughly may well prefer to see the offending officer suspended than to go through the hassle of a civil suit that would result in only a nominal monetary award. Finally, in cases involving property damage by the police, municipal insurance or contingency funds are frequently used to resolve those claims to the satisfaction of all parties. Thus, successful third party suits against the police tend to be limited to cases involving death or serious bodily injury; cases where the potential exists for a high monetary judgment.

In contrast, public employee rights have undergone enormous expansion in the last two decades. Primarily because of the federal structure of the American system of government, Congress, and to a lesser degree the courts, have left the topic of public employee rights to the individual states. For example, while private sector workers have enjoyed the right to unionize and bargain collectively with their employers since 1935, collective bargaining for police officers and sheriff's deputies is still non-existent in a dozen states. Congress has refused to approve legislation applying the National Labor Relations Act to public employees. The national legislative body has taken a similar path regarding the Occupational Safety and Health Act (OSHA) and a myriad of other labor laws.

However, court decisions have allowed some federal labor laws to be applied to public sector workers. These are the statutes and rulings that often give rise to litigation between police officers and their employers. Most important of the statutes are the Equal Employment Opportunity Act, which prohibits job discrimination based on race, color, religion, national origin, sex, pregnancy, and disability, and the Fair Labor Standards Act, which proscribes overtime compensation. Meanwhile, Supreme Court rulings regarding free speech, freedom of association, and due process have given rise to extensive public employee litigation.

While data is not available that counts the relative number of civil suits by private citizens compared to public employees, informal review of newspaper accounts and appellate court case reports suggest that litigation by employees is far more prevalent than suits brought by members of the public at large.

Areas with Prime Potential for Lawsuits

By Members of the Public
Use of Force
Vehicle Pursuits
Jail Operations
Deaths in Custody

By Agency Employees
Sex Discrimination
Race Discrimination
Adherence to Disciplinary Procedures
Overtime Compensation
Regulation of Off-Duty Conduct

Ways to Mimimize Personal Civil Liability

1. Follow agency and city/county manuals and policies. Adherence to written procedures creates a strong claim to a good faith defense.
2. Act only within the scope of your duties.
3. Act in a professional and responsible manner at all times. When faced with a difficult situation, use reason instead of emotion.
4. Know the constitutional rights of the public and respect them.
5. Know the constitutional rights of your employees and respect them.
6. Consult your legal counsel and/or superior, if any, when in doubt as to proper course of action. Document any advice given.
7. In sensitive cases, fully document your activities. Keep good written records.
8. Establish and maintain good relations with all aspects of the community.
9. Keep yourself well informed on current issues and trends in policing.
10. Keep yourself well informed on current issues in civil liability cases.

Adapted from del Carmen, *Criminal Procedure: Law and Practice (4th Edition)*, Wadsworth Publishing Company, 1998.

DISCIPLINE. "If the police are to maintain the respect and support of the public, they must deal openly and forcefully with misconduct within their own ranks whenever it occurs" (President's Commission on Campus Unrest, 1970, pages 5-8). This advice is as valid and timely as it was over thirty years ago when one considers the number of police shootings, beatings, and other criminal behavior by police officers that have been reported in the last decade. The law enforcement executive is ultimately responsible for the behavior of all personnel in his/her agency and, therefore, must establish guidelines for behavior, policies for investigating allegations of misdeeds, procedures for conducting hearings, and the disciplinary action to be taken.

One of the first steps in the disciplinary process is the determination of which employee actions will result in an internal investigation and possibly disciplinary action. Some chiefs have developed a model of behavior and potential disciplinary procedures that distinguish between errors and rule violations that are inadvertent or well-intentioned and those that are intentional and committed for personal or malicious reasons (Sheehan & Cordner, 1995). This allows the employee who is trying to do the right thing not to be punished if the behavior was well-intended but may not have conformed to current policy or practice. On the other hand, behaviors that are intentional or malicious or for personal gain must be forbidden and a system established to investigate and take disciplinary action against those employees who intentionally violate police policy and the law.

The chief must also decide who will be responsible for investigating complaints against officers and other employees. The size of the agency will dictate whether there is a separate unit or person designated for that task or if the chief executive or second in command will take on that role. No matter who is responsible for the investigation of employee misconduct, that person must report directly to and be under the control of the chief. In some agencies, there is a decentralization of investigation, the employees' direct supervisor is responsible for the investigation of minor infractions while more serious violations are investigated by the internal affairs unit. This allows the supervisor to still be responsible to direct and control her/his subordinates. If this model is adopted, copies of all complaints, investigations, findings and actions must be forwarded to the internal affairs unit so that a department depository of such complaints is kept. This ensures that an employee who has accumulated several complaints, each that may have been handled by a different supervisor, is identified and appropriate action taken.

The length of time an employee is assigned to the internal affairs unit has been debated. Some argue that due to the type of job, it should be a career appointment. Those that propose this model argue that the officer is investigating other officers and if sent back to patrol or another unit, will not receive the respect and, more importantly, the support of officers, some of whom he/she may have investigated and were subjected to disciplinary action. Others argue that appointments to the internal affairs unit should be made on a short-term basis, eight to twenty-four months, and then re-assign the officer to another unit. This allows a shorter time for the officer to make "enemies" and also allows several officers to participate in the internal affairs unit and perhaps better understand the operation and purpose of the unit.

Administrative due process should be afforded in all disciplinary hearings and actions. It has been ruled by the courts that such hearings must guarantee fairness and equity, and that constitutional protections be safeguarded. The chief must establish a procedure that meets all current legal standards in this area. As most disciplinary actions threaten either the liberty or property rights of the employee, the employee is entitled to procedural and substantive due process. By following these procedures, the disciplinary hearing and any action taken should be upheld by those who may later examine the issue.

Law enforcement executives do not want to get to the point of having to conduct employee disciplinary hearings and actions. Disciplinary actions are formal punishment and can affect the agency's morale, motivation, productivity, and environment. To avoid this, the chief must implement valid selection procedures, require on-going training, and recognize employees who perform exceptionally. Early detection and correction of problems will also help to decrease the number of problems requiring disciplinary action.

Generally, fair and consistent treatment in disciplinary matters will be supported by the employees. It is a basic expectation that improper conduct will result in some type of disciplinary action. It is when that action is unfair, inconsistent or unequal that conflicts may arise within the organization, and in some cases, within the community. Unresolved conflicts continue to grow in turmoil and ultimately become destructive to survival unless they are promptly and properly handled. The police executive who has established a system of fair and equitable discipline should experience more cooperation and a lesser need to institute discipline than one who has not established such a system.

Technology

Even though law enforcement has made great strides in technology (especially in the area of communications), the public perception of what the police can do and what the police are actually capable of doing is, in some cases, vastly different. In one agency, a dispatcher received a 911 call from a woman who stated that her kitchen was on fire and she needed the fire department. The telecommunicator confirmed the request and asked for the caller's address to which she replied: "You know the address. Stop asking questions and get them out here!" The caller then hung up! The agency did not possess an enhanced 911 system. Fortunately, the basic 911 system had a call-back feature that the telecommunicator accessed to re-establish contact with the caller. After a short discussion about the limitations of the basic 911 system, the caller gave her address so emergency units could be dispatched. As a result of the exposure of television programs and media reports regarding emergency telephone communications systems, the caller assumed that a display of the address and telephone number was directly in front of the operator as the call was answered. It is clear to see how such an expectation could have a disastrous outcome.

The expectations of citizens include the use of technologically advanced equipment and procedures. The problem is further complicated when the separation of reality and fantasy becomes distorted. In recent years, movies and television shows have used special effects in a very realistic manner. This not only increases the public's expectations but also some law enforcement leaders who observe the operation of computer-aided everything (C.A.E.) at vendor displays and exhibits at professional seminars and conferences.

Although much technological advancement has been made in the past twenty years, the law enforcement executive must ensure that the technology being considered and purchased for the department is appropriate. Most law enforcement executives are general managers, and as such, may need to seek specialized assistance when considering a new computer or information system or other technological equipment. Depending on the size of the department, an employee may be assigned this duty. In smaller agencies, or if no such employee exists, outside resources will need to be consulted, that can include specialized journals or seminars, a private consultant with experience in police technology needs, or faculty at the local university or community college.

The first step in the process should be a needs assessment to determine the specifications that the system or product should have in order to meet the agency's needs. The needs assessment should examine the goals and objectives for the system, department size, present workload, future anticipated growth, budget allocation, and other factors that will affect the type of system or product purchased. Although the assessment may be time consuming, it could prevent an agency from making costly mistakes.

After conducting the needs assessment, other agencies should be contacted about their experience concerning the product or system under consideration. The successes and failures of others can be a valuable learning tool.

Another consideration that should be made is multi-user arrangements. The court system, other law enforcement agencies, or the prosecutor's office may be considering a new computer system as well. If this is the case, the police executive may want to consider systems that are compatible so that information can be electronically exchanged. Such a jurisdiction-wide system would speed the exchange of information in areas such as warrants, arrests, detained persons, and protective orders. Additionally, agencies could take advantage of discounts due to volume buying that may not otherwise be available.

Another consideration is the operation of equipment during conditions that are less than optimum. The chief must ensure that the equipment and the system have been tested for reliability before purchasing and during installation. Regularly scheduled maintenance and testing should take place to ensure that the system remains operational. No law enforcement agency can afford equipment failure during a critical event.

Law enforcement technology encompasses many different types of hardware, software and systems including information management, computer aided dispatch, jail management, crime analysis, geographic information systems (GIS), and artificial intelligence. Information management systems are used to maintain records, master name files, incident reports, traffic citations, traffic accident reports, and may include employee information. Information is the heart of most law enforcement agencies.

All officers should be encouraged to use crime analysis to determine problems on their beats or identify patterns in crimes. Police managers can use crime analysis to determine the best allocation of personnel and to forecast future events.

Geographic information systems integrate automated database operation, crime analysis and high-level mapping. It can be used to geographically map crimes and other incidents; allow dispatchers to provide directions to emergency responders and to identify the location of such things as fire hydrants, power lines, or hazards (pipe lines, storage tanks, etc.). Investigators can use GIS for prosecution purposes, and police performance by area can be monitored.

Artificial intelligence includes the use of robots for activities such as bomb retrieval and disposal or in hostage situations. Computers are also used to investigate crimes especially those involving white-collar offenses or computers.

Computers and technology should also be incorporated into training. Not only do personnel need to be trained to use the computer programs installed at the agency, but computers should be used to provide training. Both basic and in-service training can benefit from computer-aided instruction.

In the last few years there has been a proliferation of the number of vendors who are selling technological products to law enforcement agencies. As in any other purchase, the chief executive should do his/her homework concerning the needs of the department and the ability of a system to meet those needs. Finally, the law enforcement chief executive must remember that no amount of technology replaces courteous, professional service. Employees and the public must continue to be treated with respect and fairness, and not as an appendage to the computer or other technology.

Grounds and Buildings

A new sheriff or police chief does not necessarily expect to inherit the responsibility of the maintenance of the buildings and grounds of the agency, but in some jurisdictions this is a primary responsibility of the law enforcement executive. In other jurisdictions, a unit within the governmental agency is responsible for these duties. No matter who is responsible, the chief executive needs to ensure that the buildings and grounds reflect well on the agency and on the sheriff or chief. The chief executive must make sure that various systems, i.e., heating/air, sanitation, electrical, roof, grounds, etc., are regularly inspected and that any upgrading and replacement is scheduled and budgeted for. This is especially critical if a computer upgrade is being considered. If the chief is responsible then he/she will have to make arrangements for the completion of these activities. If another unit is responsible, the sheriff or chief must work with that unit to make sure the department's buildings and grounds are maintained and that maintenance conforms to security and safety standards proscribed by the agency, especially in sensitive areas, such as the communications center or inmate housing.

The chief or sheriff is also responsible for the security of the property. In some jurisdictions this may include all buildings belonging to or leased by the jurisdiction. A procedure should be in place to ensure that this obligation is met.

Finally, as many jails and courthouses are located within the boundaries of a municipality or county, the sheriff and police chief need to work together to develop plans on responding to jail and courtroom escapes.

Court Security

Court security is a responsibility of the sheriff and a growing concern of court personnel. The sheriff must work with the judges to implement a plan that fits the needs and resources of the county. A source of valuable information is other sheriffs who have established court security procedures either in response to an incident or proactively. The Illinois Law Enforcement Training and Standards Board, the Illinois Sheriff's Association, the National Sheriff's Association, and the United States Marshall Service can provide additional information, as they have established training and other resources in this area.

Planning for a Crisis

A crisis can be any sudden event that taxes the resources of the law enforcement agency and the community. Crises can be natural or man-made events and include tornadoes, floods, snow or ice storms, terrorist acts, sensational events, or hostage situations. We all tend to think that such things "happen to the other guy." Law enforcement chief executives are no exception.

The ability of the law enforcement agency to respond to such events takes planning. The law enforcement executive must work with other agencies in the community when developing a plan for responding to a crisis, as very seldom will the event only require law enforcement response. More often than not the disaster also requires the expertise and services of other community agencies, such as the emergency management office, fire department, emergency medical services, schools, local businesses, hospitals and medical centers, Red Cross, Salvation Army, and the National Guard. Any or all of these or similar agencies may be needed if a disaster or crisis occurs, therefore it is important to involve these agencies in the planning process. For some events the emergency management agency will be primarily responsible, while for others the fire department will take control, and in still others the law enforcement agency will be in charge. Interaction and responsibilities are an important part of the plan. The plan must also identify who is authorized to initiate and terminate the crisis response. The plan must be updated, regularly reviewed by command staff, and available to potential users.

After developing the plan, testing should take place involving a disaster, crisis, or sensational incident drill. These drills will provide personnel with experience in implementing the plan and working with other agencies. The drill should be publicly announced, covered by the media, and be as realistic as possible to allow a full determination of the capabilities of the plan and agencies response. With the advent of computer simulations, more frequent drills with different scenarios can be completed which will increase personnel confidence and the ability of multiple agencies to respond and work together.

Simulated, electronic and tabletop drills must be reviewed and evaluated. As many participants as possible should be involved in the debriefing process to offer observations and comments concerning the drill and to make suggestions for changes.

Once the drill has been completed and evaluated, the plan should be rewritten to incorporate participants' comments, suggestions, and observations. Finally, command staff should review the revised plan to become familiar with the changes.

One event that many agencies may currently be ill-equipped to respond to is the sensational event. A sensational event is characterized by:

1. the unique, bizarre, or brutal nature of the event;
2. the number of persons affected and/or victims; and/or
3. the identity and/or relationship of the suspect or victim.

These situations involve strong emotions and great excitement and may result in local and national media coverage. Incidents such as the recent school shootings, hate motivated crimes and involvement of high-profile personalities stretched the resources of the local law enforcement agencies. To meet the demands of the sensational event and continue to provide services to the rest of the community, the law enforcement agency must have a well-developed, workable plan.

"Be Prepared" is the motto of the Boy Scouts and perhaps it should also be adopted by law enforcement executives. The ability to respond to a large-scale, unplanned event is vital to the safety and security of the agency and the public. A well-developed and regularly tested, evaluated, and reviewed plan will go far in preparing the agency to meet the needs of the community when a crisis event occurs.

Chapter 6

PLANNING AND BUDGETING: THE ROAD MAP FOR SUCCESS

LIKE ALL OTHER ORGANIZATIONS, police agencies will only grow and prosper with proper planning. The chief or sheriff needs to look at where the department is, where it should be and how it's going to get there. Strategic planning should involve input from many different sources–department personnel, the city manager, elected officials, and the public. Agencies should not be cynical about breadth of input–it really does bring new ideas. Also, the partners then have a stake in the successes of the planning process and are more attuned to helping achieve the goals that are set.

Within the police agency, all department members who wish to contribute should be included, from top to bottom, allowing them to buy into the future of the organization. The community's support is also needed. Publicize the plans, involve business groups, clergy, other members of the criminal justice system, homeowner associations, neighborhood groups, and other influential persons.

However, even with careful planning, wide-spread involvement and strong support, sometimes a program fails. If this is the case, a police manager should not be afraid to alter course, to make an adjustment, and to start again. Failure is not necessarily bad; however, prolonging and thus compounding a mistake could be damaging. If a program fails, it should not be covered up. Let the department, public and council know it. Tell them why it failed. An innovative agency will try many programs for each that truly works well.

Using A Budget Officer

Due to the need to continuously review the budget, if a department is large enough, a budget officer should be appointed. A chief or sheriff should be knowledgeable of the budget. But given the many time-consuming activities for the CEO, he/she really doesn't have the time to dedicate detail work to budget issues. The budget process has changed from a three-to-four-month process into a year-round process. An administrator must continuously review, analyze and revise the operating budget in order to stay current as well as be prepared for emergencies. If a department lacks an individual with requisite skills, one should be trained. An accounting background or focused budget training has become a necessity for modern public budget processes.

Budget Analysis

For at least the last thirty years, the budget process and program planning have been linked. Initially such linkage occurred under the auspices of planning programming budgeting systems (PPBS). The PPBS method involved the specification of various objectives, comparative examination of the benefits of attaining one objective over another and analysis of alternative methods or courses of action in relation to how effectively and efficiently they accomplish the objectives selected. PPBS as a system is no longer employed. It was supplanted with zero based budgeting. Zero based budgeting was supplanted in turn by performance budgeting. Now we simply refer to "budget analysis." Budget analysis requires that goals be described in sufficient detail so that they can be linked to costs. Police managers have always been involved in considerations of quality, role, mission, character, and effectiveness of their agencies. The infusion of the concept of "budget analysis" deals with the problem of translating organizational goals into financial terms. There are basically four major steps that are necessary to effect this process:

1. Identifying goals. The specific goals that are deemed appropriate will have to be selected in light of a comprehensive evaluation of needs and objectives.
2. Relating broad goals to specific programs. Specific alternative programs that may help to achieve the broad goals and objectives will then be examined in the interest of selecting those that appear most promising.
3. Relating programs to resource requirements. The specific costs of alternative programs will then be estimated in order to compare their efficiency.
4. Relating resource inputs to budget dollars. The human resources, facilities and other requirements must be translated into budget dollars–all projected several years ahead–so that the costs of the programs can be analyzed over a meaningful period.

The difference between this and prior methods is the relation of both the planning and budgeting processes to programs. Planning and budgeting historically had little relation to one another. Planning in police agencies too often consists of the development of procedures manuals. Seldom does planning involve relating agency resources to goals. Responsibility for budgeting, on the other hand, is often delegated to persons completely outside the agency, usually in city or county general administrative positions. The budget consists of line-item requests for materials or services. That is, budget categories consist of entries such as personnel salaries, building maintenance, automobile acquisition, and uniforms. This format results in a focus upon the annual increases in the budget. Major debate occurs over minor new budget items (a new computer, one additional patrol car) while thousands of dollars being spent on programs initiated years previously that have had no subsequent evaluation are ignored. In contrast, an analytic budget system forces examination of ongoing activities as well as proposed activity expansion.

Allocating costs by program (crime prevention, criminal apprehension, traffic services) results in evaluation of total organizational operations, and provides the vital link between planning and budgeting. Because 80-90 percent of police costs are attributable to salaries, the principal focus of budget analysis in law enforcement is on the utilization of police human resources–how they are distributed among the objectives and what each segment of human resources is attempting to achieve.

Such budgeting is planning oriented. Its main goal is to rationalize policy-making by providing data on the costs and benefits of alternative ways of achieving proposed objectives. What is readily apparent is the necessity of one factor–the existence of objectives. The planning process does not begin to operate with clearly defined objectives. Rather, the first phase of the planning process must consist of the formulation of operational planning objectives on the basis of somewhat ambiguous and undefined goals set by legislative groups and/or elected executives. The importance of the methodology is that, in addition to clarifying objectives, it helps move discussion away from the fairly useless absolutes of (a) what fixed amounts of money to spend no matter what the goals, and (b) what fixed objectives to achieve no matter what the costs.

Public resources are inadequate to do all the things we consider desirable and necessary. The proper role of the police administrator is viewed in this sense as that of maximizing the attainment of governmental objectives by the efficient employment of limited resources. It is not her/his function to establish a utopia, e.g., eradicate crime, prevent any civil disorder from ever occurring, cut traffic fatalities to zero.

The procedure for formulating operational planning objectives consists of transforming broad goals into tangible terms where the degree of achievement can be observed and measured. What results are successive levels of objectives from goal statements specifying the broad, grand design of the organization, to strategic objectives, to operational objectives, to specific performance criteria.

Analysis of Program Alternatives

Analysis of program alternatives is the most problematic aspect of applying budget analysis to police management. Such analysis first of all requires an assessment of program effectiveness. With the exception of a very few patrol distribution studies, we totally lack data regarding the effectiveness of various police programs.

We do not know, for instance, the differential effect of crime suppression activities (uniform patrol) on crime rates as contrasted to criminal apprehension activities (investigative follow-up). Thus, the allocative decisions in relation to attaining the broad goal of crime control are now made on the basis of judgments relating primarily to workload demands.

For instance, detective divisions typically operate on the principle that every crime reported ought to be investigated to the exhaustion of substantial leads. Whenever the workload generated by this operating principle exceeds the capability of assigned personnel, the investigative unit is typically assigned additional personnel as soon as they are available, i.e., budgeted by jurisdictional management. We have failed to examine, however, the effectiveness of this basic operating principle in relation to control of crime rates. In other words, there have been no attempts to study the effect of "investigating" only those individual crimes with a very high probability of being cleared by arrest, and ignoring all others. (Public pressure to investigate all crimes to exhaustion is a factor here, but merits a separate analysis.)

Such a decision might dramatically alter the allocation of resources, and allow greater emphasis on crime suppression. Or, we might do precisely the opposite, reallocating resources devoted to suppression to criminal investigation by reaching a decision to cease most patrol for purposes of controlling, for instance, business burglaries. The resources that were previously required for this type of patrol could then be assigned to the criminal apprehension function, e.g., surveillance of known burglars or even investigation of other types of offenses. However, we do not know which of these would be an appropriate reallocation in relation to lowering crime rates without research studies. In other words, the differential effectiveness of alternative police programs that address similar objectives has not been established.

An additional example might help clarify this point. Let us suppose that a police manager faces a decision to implement one of two programs. The first will vastly expand the criminal laboratory facilities of his agency and train a number of evidence technicians for field assignment. The second will initiate a legal advisory unit in the agency that will provide several attorneys to assist officers in the preparation of cases. The appropriate alternative ought to be the program that will have the most effect on crime rates (or crime clearance rates as an intermediate factor). Unfortunately, we have no data regarding the comparative effects of these programs, nor even illuminating related data such as the comparative importance of physical versus testimonial evidence as they affect crime clearance. Genuine cost effective analysis is thus impossible.

The problem of determining program effects is complicated by the fact that police organizational units do not produce mutually exclusive and exhaustive categories of outputs. For instance, two of the most important police outputs, crime suppression and traffic regulation, are almost always "concurrent products" of a patrol division. That is, a cruising patrol unit is at the same time suppressing crime and preventing traffic violations. We therefore encounter a serious problem whenever attempts are made to "cost out" these programs. Specifically, the problem is deciding what portion of the costs of operating a cruising patrol unit ought to be charged to crime (or traffic) control. The costing-out process is, of course, absolutely necessary if we are to analyze the appropriateness of various alternative programs. Attempts at comparing the cost-effectiveness, to use the previous example, of crime suppression versus criminal apprehension, are meaningless if we cannot identify the costs of crime suppression.

And that is not the end of the complications. There is the additional problem of deciding upon the program area to which the costs of certain police activities ought to be charged. We all readily recognize that a "hot domestic," if rapid intervention does not occur, often results in a criminal offense. Similarly, an intoxicated person in an alley represents a criminal hazard in both the sense of potential offender and victim. Categorizing the costs of police activities to control domestics, public intoxication and the like exclusively to public service distorts analysis of crime control costs. Similarly, the analysis of subprogram emphasis within the crime control program is complicated due to exigencies such as the fact that many activities of a juvenile division are often difficult to categorize in exclusive terms of crime prevention, crime suppression, or criminal apprehension.

Thus, there are a number of factors that complicate attempts to compare the cost-effectiveness of alternative police programs. The present state of the art enables us to establish a police "programmatic" budget. However, we are not currently able to initiate a genuine budget analysis system. Such a system requires that various alternative courses of action be analyzed as to their cost effectiveness in achieving stipulated objectives. Research has not yet produced information that would allow such analysis.

However, even a programmatic budget, albeit without extensive systems analysis, still provides considerable insight regarding the nature of aggregate expenditures. It is a useful aspect of a managerial information system and ought to be implemented. It does not replace the line-item budget but is certainly a meaningful supplement.

Budget Process

The actual expenditures (line-item) for the current and previous years are inevitably the starting point for both the chief and the finance director/administrator. The chief has to justify any change based upon known cost increases, projected cost increases or for possible additional programs. A budget should be projected three to five years into the future, correlated with goals as noted above, and specify the resources needed to reach those goals. It is necessary to know the history of the municipality or county, the population of projected annexations, and/or growth and the political desires for growth.

All labor contracts have significant budget implications. A department can encounter problems funding wage and benefit increases if they are not provided in the budget. Although wages and benefits are usually negotiated by the financial director or administrator, indirect compensation such as clothing allowances, overtime and court appearance compensation can have a substantial impact on budget planning. Given that 80–90 percent of a police budget is personnel expenses, there is not a lot of cushion for agency operational costs.

A perennial argument is whether or not to inflate budget requests. The argument for an inflated budget is that the government entity will cut the budget anyway, and by inflating the initial request, the chief or sheriff will end up with the financing they wanted to start with. The opposite argument is that an inflated budget destroys credibility with city managers, finance departments, and government boards. Most seasoned police managers would argue that by being consistent and reasonable, sooner or later an agency will obtain what it needs. If a chief or sheriff has a reputation for fair, accurate, consistent and honest requests, it will pay off in the long run. If a chief or sheriff is known to consistently inflate requests, then he/she can gain a reputation for not being serious in department requests, and the department may suffer more drastic cutbacks.

SHERIFF'S BUDGET. A sheriff's budget process is different than most local municipal processes. The budget has both internal and external dynamics. Externally, constituents expect a lean operation that will still provide all the services promised during campaigning. Internally, the sheriff is expected to provide the tools for the proper running of the operation, to maximize safety and effectiveness in the organization. Employees expect nothing less. There is obvious stress in meeting both sets of demands.

The sheriff's budget reflects the several responsibilities of the office of sheriff, including law enforcement, officer of the court, court security, jail/corrections, dispatching, civil process, inmate transportation, and building custodian. These can become major issues during elections for office. The elected official needs to carefully monitor and stay abreast of the budget status. The sheriff should explain unexpected expenses created by emergency situations such as major incidents/cases and disasters. The sheriff must document each of these occurrences for future responses. The citizens of the county need to understand how the expenses contributed to safety and security.

Relating to Community-Wide Needs

It is important in any type of organization to plan and articulate goals, objectives, mission statements, philosophical views, operational issues, and programs to citizens and employees. They need to gain understanding of what, why, who, when, and how much this vision is going to cost and what are the benefits. Consensus and support are ultimately the final determination on success in budgeting. The days of a police chief or sheriff operating as an independent entity within city/county government are gone. In municipalities, the advent of city manager government has significantly contributed to the chief of police being expected to be one of the "players" on the city management team. Some department heads rebel against the team concept and the articulation of a departmental goals and objectives program within the community-wide context. A more realistic position is:

- Embrace the goals and objectives program as a means of "showcasing" the police department.
- Do not set goals wholly based upon achievements requiring financial support.

- Submit the budget within the parameters and/or financial constraints set forth for the budget year.
- Always attach an addendum to the budget outlining new ideas and costing out proposed programs that can be delivered should funding become available in the subsequent year.

Employing this format, the chief or sheriff operates within community-wide priorities (or creates law enforcement related priorities for the community), functions as a team player and gives city/county management a role to play in ensuring that public safety issues are paramount in the budget process.

Budget Justification

Goal-oriented, multi-year budgeting allows the organization to plan for future service demands and capital requirements. A budget that includes the current fiscal year, as well as the next three fiscal years, allows for careful planning of programs and facilities. Goal-oriented budgeting requires the administrator to think "three to five years out." This practice also helps to balance projected revenues with projected expenditures. This planning encourages elected officials to think "forward" and discourages their involvement in routine day-to-day expenditures.

No matter what the format of the budget, the executive must provide justification for the requests. Even though the budget process is not premised on a "zero-based" format, one must be prepared to document and justify requests. Justification can be supported with a short historical chronology. "Show 'em where you've been and tell 'em where you're headed," an old time budget officer once said. Part of the justification can relate the economies accomplished in the past, coupled with future goals. With employment of visual aids and computer generated graphs the budget presentation can be part of the "selling of the budget." This is particularly true at the stage of city council/board review. Council/board members are essentially laypersons representing a wide cross-section of the community, with limited time to devote to "figuring out" the budget. The budget presentation should be easy to understand, direct, logically presented, and visual.

Examples and demonstrations will go a long way toward making a case for the needs of the department:

- What better way to demonstrate the need for lap-top computers than to plug into an overhead projector and display a presentation directly from computer files?
- Utilize a vendor's short video presentation of a much-needed product for the department (semi-automatic weapons, in-car video cameras, mobile data systems, etc).

Demonstrations must always be brief. But a concise demonstration can be very effective.

The law enforcement administrator who seeks the support of elected officials wants to make an effective presentation. But standing before elected officials who are charged with providing all the community's needs and utilizing scare tactics to justify an increased budget is an unwise approach. A chief or sheriff who warns of frighteningly high crime rates and dangerous neighborhoods is risking a career. Elected officials want to hear of successes whenever possible. Alarming numbers should always be qualified and reasoning offered that is honest and appropriate. Support is secured or strengthened by the interest and endorsement of neighborhood groups and homeowners' associations. Meeting with these special interest groups in advance of budget hearings and explaining department needs is a form of community policing.

Sources of Revenue

One must recognize that municipal budgets rely heavily upon sales tax and user revenues that require aggressive economic development strategies in order to bring jobs to the community. A good administrator will commit police department resources toward assisting the city officials in attracting business and industry to the community.

The police department has a legitimate role in the strategy of the economic development process. Police personnel should support community-wide initiatives. Visiting business executives are impressed by an active, community-involved police department.

One Illinois chief assisted in hosting a group of Japanese executives on their visit to his city. The lake patrol was under police department jurisdiction. The chief escorted the group in the patrol boats for a view of some of the city infrastructure from the water. He was able to recall some conversational Japanese from his military service. This so impressed the visitors that they ultimately moved a corporate entity to the city. Police managers should not underestimate the influence they might have on economic development.

GIFTS. Unsought and unplanned gift opportunities often come from community groups and foundations. Seeking community grants can be incorporated into totality of "public relations" duties of a chief executive. Public service presentations can be excellent opportunities to gain financial support for a K-9 unit, specialized investigative equipment, youth programming or other needs that can be met with one-time purchases, and/or program development costs. Obviously, some subtlety is required.

GRANTS. One method of meeting needs when traditional revenue sources are inadequate is through grant funding. However, there are obligations associated with acceptance of grant funds. A common stipulation is that once the grant is expired, the program must continue with local funding. Additional personnel who are hired through grant programs cannot be furloughed at grant expiration according to the terms of most federal and state programs.

Grants generally prohibit "supplanting." A traffic enforcement program which has already been budgeted and approved, for example, would not qualify for most grant programs. However, the Department of Transportation might approve a request from a municipality that is unable to finance such a unit, but is able to demonstrate a need.

Grant funding often raises ethical questions. Is the jurisdiction truly unable to fund the program without grant assistance? Is the jurisdiction actually committed to employ a funded program only as proposed? Will it truly continue funding beyond the grant life or hide a reduction in funding somewhere else in the budget? The governmental body to which a chief or sheriff reports should be thoroughly briefed on any effort to obtain grant funds. Grants are not always "free money." Acceptance generally represents both an immediate and continuing financial obligation. This is especially important with regard to the hiring of additional personnel. One reason politicians are reluctant to hire new employees is the fear that a changing fiscal picture could force layoffs. Any layoff or furlough is politically unpopular with labor organizations and the public at large.

Chapter 7

EMPLOYEE ASSOCIATIONS

MANY POLICE MANAGERS SINCERELY BELIEVE that attempting to deal cordially with employee associations is about as productive as running headlong into a brick wall. Experiences over a period of years can easily leave a police manager cynical and jaded. Unions are not easy to deal with in any organizational context. They certainly are not easy to deal with in an environment as politically charged and volatile as law enforcement. The situation is not impossible. But it would be naive to suggest that a warm and fuzzy relationship can be created, then maintained for years. It is not in the nature of the beast.

It is important for police managers to understand the political and social dynamics of employee organizations. Union officials and staff are elected or paid to be advocates for officers. A "good working relationship" with management will assist in realizing this goal. However, perceptions that there is a "cozy" relationship with management will almost inevitably backfire on union officials and staff.

With rare exceptions, once a union official is perceived as too close to management, their tenure is short lived. Employee association members seek assurance that they will be vigorously represented in both grievance and contract negotiations. Their worst fear is being "sold out" by union officials. Thus, from a political perspective if union officials want to remain in office, they are required to maintain an adversarial posture with management. And it must be noted that many union officials want very badly to remain in office.

Being an officer in an employee association is not entirely an onerous hassle. There is a reasonable amount of status and prestige associated with such positions. Further, for a street patrol officer, there is a political/social life available that otherwise would never be tasted. Police union officials from major cities, such as Chicago, are routinely invited to legislative signings on the White House lawn. They receive phone calls from U.S. Senators and congressional representatives. They attend social functions sponsored by the governor. While on business trips, they stay at the best conference class hotels, with reasonably generous expense accounts. In short, a patrol officer working the midnight shift on a beat may suddenly be catapulted onto the national political stage. And we can hardly blame her/him for wanting to stay there.

The situation may not be nearly as dramatic in small communities. But the principle holds. Anyone who has held a position of responsibility in a union will certainly tell you that it's not all garden parties. The hassles are indeed many. But at the same time it is not all hassles.

It should come as no surprise to a police chief or sheriff, then, that union officials often appear unnecessarily to seek controversy and confrontation. If they want to stay in office, they must be perceived as uncompromising advocates for their clientele. They must be perceived as no-nonsense, tough, "we aren't going to take this anymore," representatives for the rank and file. The need to "fan the fires" is real.

That does not mean that the situation has to degenerate to a long string of bitter battles. An analogous relationship is that between a state's attorney and defense counsel. They do not, as a norm, hate one another. They do not do everything in their power to embarrass or humiliate one another. Indeed, frequently they will walk out of the courthouse and have coffee together. However, it is understood by all parties that the formal relationship is inherently an adversarial one. Both parties are duty bound to represent their clientele appropriately. That can and should be done professionally, operating within a set of understood rules. And attorneys from either side who violate that code of conduct lose in the long run. They no longer can obtain reasonable cooperation from their counterparts, are not trusted and are less successful.

Police managers need to strive to establish a solid working relationship with union officials, the same kind of relationship that professional state and defense attorneys cultivate with one another. It is respectful, even friendly. But it is not warm and fuzzy.

Developing Relationships

Even though police administrators may practice the best management techniques, employees may still organize an association. Reasons include militant employees, poor supervision, and actions of city/county management or city councils. More than any other factor, however, is money. Data support the perception that organized public employees are better off economically than those who are not. If organization of employees is inevitable, a chief or sheriff should not despair. They need to preserve management rights and maintain strong leadership.

Once an association is established, there is no single set of "rules of conduct" that applies to every situation. A positive working relationship in a rural county in Illinois may involve dynamics impossible to maintain in Cook County. Expectations and adjustments are necessary simply because of variation in personality among police managers and union officials. What works during one time frame may not work when there is a change of leadership. Thus, anything said in this respect must be regarded as generic guidelines, not a blueprint.

Some police officials have been successful in incorporating employee associations formally in staff participation roles. Other police officials have been more successful in involving a cross-section of staff in decision-making processes, but not under the auspices of official employee association representation.

A good grievance system should be in place ensuring that there are channels open for employees to properly grieve any fancied or real unfairness. Employees must feel there is a system in place where their rights can be assured. Many grievances can be rectified at the unit level in a satisfactory manner. This can be accomplished if first line supervisors have the ability to settle minor problems. However, if differences cannot be solved at the unit level, then employees must be allowed a route to the chief's office. A well-written and publicized grievance system is a must if a police chief or sheriff is to show proper leadership and maintain a non-hostile work environment.

Police managers must stay cognizant of the association's chain of command. Just as a police manager would not appreciate union officials going around the police agency's chain, good relationships demand that the union chain of command be acknowledged.

The setting of meetings with union officials is often symbolically important. The chief's office is not necessarily the best place to hold such meetings. Although a police chief or sheriff may be perfectly comfortable there, union officials may not. Other settings within an agency are certainly possible. Further, many police managers have been more successful in meeting for lunch at a local restaurant, or using other informal settings. Structured negotiations on sensitive issues are probably not appropriate in such settings, but a free floating discussion of agency initiatives and policies may well be.

If a police chief or sheriff is successful in establishing a solid working relationship with union officials, the issue of "informal understandings" will inevitably arise. This is an inevitable scenario because the public posturing of both management and labor does not necessarily represent their final position. There are certainly issues that represent "a line in the sand" or "a ditch to die in." But there are other issues that are not so critical. Or there may be an issue that is extremely important to one side, but not necessarily to the other. This is the source of informal understandings. Put in simple vernacular, such understandings usually take the form, "If you give me this one, I'll give you one downstream." Publicly, however, it is in no one's interest to formally state that this is the understanding. Critics of this process would label it "secret deals." And such understandings are indeed fraught with potential danger. But it would be naive to suggest that they are uncommon. Further, it would be naive to suggest that they should never be a part of the working relationship with an employee association. A statement like, "I am going to oppose this in front of city council, but I understand that it's important to you," is said everyday. Caution is certainly in order, but it is not inherently unethical to convey that one issue is more important to a manager than another.

The Morale Issue

Darrel Stephens, former executive director of the Police Executive Research Forum, once observed that he never walked into a police department and visited with patrol officers without being told that, "Morale has never been lower." It does indeed seem to be an axiom of police work that morale is always perceived to be lower than it used to be, and never good. There have been numerous analytic reviews of the phenomenon. Much of the research has been done under the auspices of examining stress in policing. Formal research indicates that internal, administrative stress is rated by officers as more problematic than the stress generated by dealing with the public. Certainly, managers should strive to create an optimistic, healthy atmosphere. But police managers should also recognize that what was true in the 1800s may well always be true—"A policeman's lot is not a happy one."

The morale problem is related to the issue of "who polices the police." The question of "who polices the police" in a democratic society is not simple to answer. In the United States, by and large, our response has been police chiefs and sheriffs. That is, we have consciously insulated the police from partisan political influence, and as such, depend upon police management to perform a function that might otherwise be done by someone in general municipal or county administration. Thus, some level of stress is inevitable between police management and line officers. Whether that stress is out of hand, and indeed morale has never been lower, is an important issue. Police managers should endeavor to monitor employee attitudes.

Monitoring trend data regarding several indirect indicators of morale may be helpful. The rate of grievances filed may be affected by a number of factors, but general morale is potentially one. Agencies with poor employee attitudes typically experience much higher sick leave rates than those with positive interaction. Resignations are rare enough in all agencies, particularly smaller ones, that they are problematic as a measure of morale. Nevertheless, a police chief or sheriff should be cognizant of whether those rates are what would normally be expected. Frequently, transfer applications are also an indicator of poor morale. Again, other factors may affect this statistic, but general morale should be considered.

> **Observations on Good Employee Relations**
>
> - Police administrators should strive to eliminate the adoption of trade union labels to describe police officers; such as, "rank and file", "shop/shift stewards", "labor", "management". These terms tend to separate officers and create divisions between police officers, supervisors/command officers, and administrators.
>
> - Dialogue should be maintained throughout the year, not just in anticipation of/or during contract negotiations.
>
> - There should be recognition up and down the chain of command that change is threatening to people. Consequently, change should never be attempted without an implementation strategy that is "user friendly".
>
> - Administrators should recognize that employees have insight and contributions to offer concerning policy, projects and departmental budgets. A philosophy should prevail that asks the person doing the job how best it could be improved, and to a greater extent, how that improvement will contribute to the overall mission of the department.
>
> - Listen to employees who complain or suggest improvements in "creature comforts", i.e., squad car maintenance/markings/identification; small equipment needs; small enhanced safety measures or equipment; uniform or shoulder patch enhancements; break areas; training suggestions.
>
> - For years, one department had officers wearing a stock off-the-shelf shoulder patch with the name of the city on it. They reacted to a call for change by accepting drawings submitted from the officers for a new patch. As a result of several submissions, a combination patch was collaboratively designed which individualized the department. The acceptance was unanimous and eventually lead to the patch being incorporated on the squad cars.

Employee surveys have been used by some organizations to help measure morale. However, they are expensive to conduct and may engender a cynical response. The recognized strategy of management by walking around, "MBWA," is another technique. Police managers employing this strategy need to be careful, however, that they do not engender routine circumventing of the chain of command. A police chief or sheriff should expect that supervisors and middle managers will be threatened by their presence and conversations with subordinates. If MBWA is to be employed, then it should be preceded by careful understanding with supervisors about what will become of the feedback obtained. Some managers have found it more effective to identify certain "benchmark" persons with whom they routinely confer regarding issues and problems in the agency. An obvious cautionary note is to be sure that the feedback obtained is representative and not self-serving.

Finally, it should be noted that there will always be a perceptual lag between the true state of employee relations and reports of morale. Old grievances die slowly. Employees who have not been treated well in the past will not overnight report that everything is fine. The lag time is probably not in decades, but it is certainly at least in months and often in years.

Collective Bargaining

Perceptions regarding the appropriate role of a police chief or sheriff in the collective bargaining process varies to the extremes. There are some police managers who are adamant that they are involved as full participants in the collective bargaining process. There are others who are just as adamant that they should not be involved at all. Whether directly "sitting at the table" or not, there are certain guidelines that exist.

First, the police chief or sheriff must be concerned about the protection of management rights. The importance of preserving management rights cannot be overstated. Further, whether negotiating the very first collective bargaining agreement or the twentieth agreement, management rights are always at risk. Union negotiators will endeavor to acquire as much of a role in the operational decisions of the agency as possible. Once given away, management rights, if they can be reacquired at all, will be bought back at a heavy price (literally–as economic concessions). It must also be understood that the economic package may be far more important to the negotiator for the city or county than the law enforcement agency's management rights. A young negotiator moving up the career ladder will, in particular, be more prone to give away management rights than a senior member of the permanent city or county staff. It is in their interest to obtain the best possible economic package. The fact that management rights are given away in order to do so will never appear on their resumè. Thus, police managers must be vigilant to see to it that directly or indirectly management rights are not signed away.

> A few months ago, I ran into a friend who was a long-time chief. I inquired as to how things were going, knowing that his department had a strong militant union, and they had just signed a new contract after long and hectic negotiations. My friend said, "Great, I come into the office in the morning, sign my name a few times, read the local paper, and then go home." I asked, "How come?" He replied, "I lost some more of my management rights, so I manage very little anymore."

A collective bargaining agreement is a complex legal document. It is easy to inadvertently sign away management rights. For example, a "maintenance of standards" clause, holding simply that *if a modification in working conditions is not stipulated in the contract, the same conditions as previously existed will pertain throughout the life of the contract,* can be catastrophic. In extreme situations police managers have found that they could not change the color of patrol cars because of a maintenance of standards clause. An enumeration of what constitutes working conditions should be included. Seniority clauses must be carefully drawn, or a manager will find that they are unable to assign personnel at will. Managers have found themselves unable to adjust staffing levels across shifts because certain contract clauses were naively included. A professional negotiator cognizant of these nuances should be part of the management collective bargaining team.

> **Management Rights**
>
> a. To determine agency mission, policies, and to set forth all standards of service offered to the public;
>
> b. To plan, direct, control, schedule and determine the operations or services to be conducted by employees of the City/County;
>
> c. To determine the methods, means, number and ranks of personnel needed to carry out the agency's mission, including hireback details;
>
> d. To direct the working forces;
>
> e. To hire, promote, assign, or transfer employees;
>
> f. To suspend, discipline or discharge for just cause (just cause not required for probationary employees);
>
> g. To lay-off or relieve employees;
>
> h. To make and enforce rules and regulations;
>
> i. To introduce new or improved methods, equipment, or facilities;
>
> j. To contract out for goods and services; and
>
> k. To take any and all actions as may be necessary to carry out the mission of the City/County and the Department in situations of civil emergency conditions as may be declared.

Police chiefs or sheriffs may find themselves in an uncomfortable position with regard to economic demands of the employee association. On the one hand, they may be sympathetic to increasing wages and benefits of their staff. On the other hand, they concurrently play the role of one department manager on a city or county team. The vast majority of professionals in the field of public sector labor relations would suggest that a departmental manager not participate in economic negotiations. They should adopt the public stance of suggesting that "my officers deserve as much money as the jurisdiction can possibly afford to provide them." In many jurisdictions, even if a representative of the police department sits on the management collective bargaining team, they do not participate in caucuses regarding economic issues. Professional negotiators recognize the conflict of interest position that a representative of the agency is in. Some representatives of the city or county negotiation team may be anxious to enlist the support of a police chief or sheriff on economic issues. A police manager would be well advised to be adamant about remaining neutral on these issues.

Chapter 8

COMMUNITY-ORIENTED POLICING: "FULL SERVICE" LAW ENFORCEMENT

In 1829, the English Parliament passed the Metropolitan Police Act in which Sir Robert Peel proposed that the principal objective of the police was the prevention of crime (Radzinowicz, 1968). Later, Peel wrote the police are the public and the public are the police and that the power of the police to fulfill their duties depended on public approval of their actions (Radzinowicz, 1968). Over 170 years later, the police in the United States are still practicing these principles and have used them to advance community-oriented policing. There is much argument concerning community-oriented policing, whether it is old wine in a new bottle, a philosophy, a program or a fad soon to go the way of the hula hoop. But whatever the critics and opponents label it, police agencies throughout the country have overwhelmingly adopted this style of policing. Some agencies have done so as a department-wide philosophy while others have instituted special teams responsible for specific programs.

The purpose of this chapter is to discuss community-oriented policing as it relates to enduring, surviving and thriving as a law enforcement executive. Gary Cordner's model of community policing will be used to examine issues relating to community-oriented policing such as role expectations, accountability, citizen involvement, decentralization, and the role of arrest. Finally, the problems that may be created by community-oriented policing will be discussed.

Defining Community-Oriented Policing

Trying to define community-oriented policing is like trying to store gelatin in a colander. No matter how hard one tries, it escapes and creates problems. There is no easy definition of community-oriented policing to give to a council member or media representative. Some describe it as a philosophy, while others name specific programs or projects. The "father" of community policing, Robert Trojanowicz, felt compelled to publish Ten Principles of Community Policing to clarify his vision of community policing. More recently, Gary Cordner (1999) proposed a model of community policing that is composed of the following four dimensions:

- Philosophical;
- Strategic;
- Tactical; and,
- Organizational.

Each of these dimensions and their elements will be used as a cornerstone of discussion for the implementation of community-oriented policing.

Philosophical Dimension

It is often argued that community-oriented policing is a philosophy and, therefore, should be instituted as such. Cordner (1999) defines the philosophical dimension as "the central ideas and beliefs underlying community policing." The law enforcement executive instituting community-oriented policing through the adoption of a department-wide philosophy should include citizen input, broad police function, and personal service as the underpinnings of this dimension (Cordner, 1999). Citizens in a free society need to have access and input to the police. This is done through elected officials, community organizations, neighborhood groups, and special interest groups. An open dialog with these groups allows the police to know the concerns and issues facing the citizens they serve. Some agencies accomplish this through neighborhood meetings, citizen advisory boards, open forums, radio and television call-in shows, community surveys, and other formal and informal means. Many of these activities allow input from citizens who are not members of an organization or association and who should not be compelled to join in order to be heard.

A second element of the philosophical dimension is broad police function. This includes not only the crime prevention, crime fighting and law enforcement functions of the police, but also contributing to quality of life, general assistance and social service roles. As the police are the 24-hour, 365-day-a-year service providers of the community, the agency and its officers must be able to meet the needs of the citizens when called upon to do so. These include social service and other quality of life activities that the police, at one time, did not consider important, but are the things that affect citizens daily. Such activities include illegally parked vehicles, abandoned vehicles, loud groups of young adults, unlit street lights and graffiti. This broad police function goes hand in hand with personal service, another element of the philosophical dimension. Personal service is really personalized service to the community and neighborhood. It includes assigning officers to the same beat or area for a long period of time.

Targeted enforcement and other crime specific efforts are needed in some neighborhoods, especially when first implementing community-oriented policing. This approach is proactive, targeted enforcement with clearly defined intervention strategies, aimed at particular offenses, committed by particular offenders at specific places and times. Crime control is the central objective. In this way "the predators" are taken off the street so that other services can be instituted (Hoover, 1999).

The police agency must work with the citizens of each neighborhood to determine the needs of that neighborhood and assist the residents in meeting those needs. Additionally, the police must continuously monitor the tactics used to ensure that each neighborhood is receiving the most effective police service at a particular point in time. As the needs of the community change so should the tactics and programs of the police. In order to accomplish this evolution of community-oriented policing in neighborhoods, police tactics should be reviewed regularly, both internally and externally, and changes implemented as the needs of the neighborhood warrant. This co-production of police services and community needs should result in the citizens taking back their neighborhoods and sharing the responsibility for continued order and preservation.

In order to provide continuity in the policing of the neighborhoods, officers should be deployed in such a way that they are assigned to a particular beat or neighborhood in long-term or permanent assignments. These assignments should be in proactive partnership with citizens to identify and solve neighborhood problems. This allows officers to become familiar with citizens in the area, as well as allowing citizens to get to know officers who are assigned to their neighborhood. As officers and citizens become acquainted with each other, citizens will develop a relationship with officers that may result in more information being relayed concerning crimes and incidents. As officers become familiar with the neighborhood residents, they will discover those gatekeepers of the community who know other members of the neighborhood, can provide information and can mobilize residents to action. Additionally, officers can work with the residents to identify problems and implement long-term solutions.

Fortunately, this approach also represents classic job enrichment. Officers are given "ownership" of a neighborhood. Ownership is important, as people will invest in themselves quicker than in others (Braiden, 1992). Braiden captures the importance of "ownership" in all elements of human enterprise through his article titled "Who Paints a Rented House?" Officers who are given ownership of a beat will more likely work with residents to identify and resolve neighborhood problems. When citizens see officers assigned to their neighborhood and working with them, they then feel a bond and will work with the officer.

At the same time, law enforcement executives must be watchful for those citizens and officers who claim too much ownership in each other. Some police agencies have encountered resistance when reassigning officers or seeking changes in assignments. In some instances community groups have lobbied city council members in order to keep a particular officer in the neighborhood. This can affect work schedules and employee allocation, as well as officer career development. Strategies must be developed to overcome such resistance.

In assigning permanent officers to beats, the chief executive must be cognizant of the need for jurisdiction-wide coverage. Some agencies have implemented a specialized neighborhood beat team, while other officers respond to radio calls. Other agencies have fully implemented permanent neighborhood/beat assignments in which officers, when not answering calls, are assigned to their beat to work on problems or to contact residents.

To recover resources for community policing efforts, many agencies adopt differential response. Calls that demand immediate response are given priority, other calls are answered by the beat officer assigned to that neighborhood as time permits, and still other calls are handled over the telephone and a report made. If differential response is undertaken by the police agency, the call taker should explain to the citizen the response that will be made and the reason for that response. If a citizen still insists on seeing an officer, then one should be sent and the citizen given an estimated time of arrival for the officer. If the officer is unable to make the appointment due to an emergency, then the citizen should be re-contacted and told of the delay.

It is the responsibility of police leaders to develop the community-oriented policing philosophy in the department. The chief executive must be actively involved in obtaining citizen and agency input, broadening the police function and personalizing service throughout the agency. The old adage "what you do speaks much louder than what you say" is particularly relevant when implementing and sustaining community-oriented policing. Only when the elements of the philosophical dimension are incorporated throughout the department will they become the way that policing is done.

Strategic Dimension

The strategic dimension includes "the key operational concepts that translate philosophy into action. These strategic concepts are the links between the broad ideas and beliefs that underlie community policing and specific programs and practices by which it is implemented" (Cordner, 1999). Reoriented operations, geographic focus and an emphasis on prevention are some of the elements of the strategic dimension.

One of the tenets of community-oriented policing is the replacement of isolating or ineffective operational practices. The advent of motorized patrol and the development of the two-way radio allowed police to be mobile and to traverse a greater distance while on duty. This also had the effect of isolating the officer, causing the officer to remain in the vehicle and close to the radio in order to respond to calls rapidly. Rapid response was thought to increase the chances of apprehending criminal offenders; however, studies have not found that to be true (see Eck, 1983; Greenwood and Petersilia, 1975; and Kelling, et al., 1974). In recent years the idea that all incidents must be answered immediately has been challenged, and other options have been instituted by police agencies. While true emergencies must still receive rapid response, other calls can be answered using differential response.

Some agencies have also reexamined the way investigations are being conducted. The beat officer is responsible for conducting more follow-up investigations, while detectives conduct investigations only when the offense meets certain criteria. Additionally, some agencies are creating investigative teams that concentrate on offenders, not offenses. Some agencies encourage detectives to examine the investigations they handle or the repeat offenders they arrest to identify problems. The investigators then implement problem-solving and crime prevention strategies.

Another element of the strategic dimension is geographic focus. Not only are officers geographically assigned for long periods of time, but the analysis of crimes and calls for service is done geographically. Under traditional policing, officers and supervisors were held accountable for their beat or area only during the time they were present and were assigned a different area each time they were on duty. In other words, the officer was expected to keep things quiet during his/her shift. Under community-oriented policing officers are assigned a small geographical area and are expected to know what occurred in that area even when not on duty. If a problem pattern develops, they are expected to tackle the underlying issue.

However, no officer is on duty 24 hours a day, 7 days a week, nor do we want them to be. To resolve this dilemma, police agencies have instituted different programs depending on their resources and community-oriented policing strategy. Some agencies may develop a team of community-oriented policing specialist officers who work a sector but do not respond to calls. Other agencies assign officers to small geographic areas in order to identify and work on long-term problems, when not responding to calls for service in a larger area. Finally, other agencies assign a group of officers to a geographic area. This group is responsible for 24-hour coverage of the area including responding to calls and long-term problem solving. Generally, if an agency falls in the latter two cases the agency has instituted differential response as part of their policing strategy. Additionally, some agencies have assigned investigators in the same manner as patrol officers, assigning them to a geographic area to investigate most crimes occurring in that area. Some crimes, such as murder and motor vehicle theft, may still be investigated by detectives who specialize in that particular offense.

Crime prevention and a proactive orientation is another element of the strategic dimension. This element encourages officers to conscientiously move from being strictly reactive to examining incidents for patterns and underlying problems. They are responsible for "directed patrol," using crime patterns and information about people on the beat to identify problems and develop solutions. This involves information gathering, citizen contact and working with the residents to determine problems and develop and implement solutions.

Officers should not only be given the responsibility to take such action but also provided the support to do so. This includes the ability to contact and work with other departments and agencies to solve problems. To accomplish this, leaders in the police agency must have paved the way with those agencies, explaining what the police officers are doing and asking for their cooperation. By having all agencies in the municipality involved in community-oriented policing, problem-solving efforts will be more effective. Community-oriented service is institutionalized throughout the municipality or county. In some jurisdictions this may be informally done and in others a more formal structure between agencies must be developed.

Tactical Dimension

Programs, practices and behaviors must be developed to carry out the philosophic and strategic dimensions that are permeating the police agency. This is the tactical dimension in Cordner's model and "ultimately translates ideas, philosophies, and strategies into concrete programs, practices, and behaviors" (Cordner, 1999). The core elements of this dimension include positive interaction, partnerships and problem solving.

Members of the police agency must make every effort to have positive interactions with the citizens they serve. This must be done by every employee who has contact with the public. Time must be invested by all employees to develop positive interactions with those they serve. This can be done as easily as listening to the person and responding appropriately by giving assistance or referrals as needed. The police officer should respond to calls for service not just as an enforcer of the law but as an opportunity to interact positively, identify problems, and provide quality service. The officers should be encouraged to get out of their patrol vehicles when not responding to calls and talk to the citizens they serve. They should interact with the people in public places such as parks, businesses, schools, and parking lots. They should talk to citizens who are in their yards or on the sidewalk. In this manner, the police officer will get to know those citizens who live, work, and do business in the officer's beat. This in turn should allow the officer to develop contacts who can assist the officer to solve problems, including criminal incidents. Citizens become familiar with their neighborhood officer(s) and will be more willing to come forward with information and assistance when needed. This information can provide the basis that the officer needs to effectuate an arrest. Additionally, this interaction between police officers and citizens will allow community members to understand the role of and need for arrest.

One of the cornerstones of community-oriented policing is participation of citizens with the police to identify and correct problems. These partnerships range from formal activities such as citizen patrol, community clean-ups, attendance at the citizen police academy, publication of a neighborhood newsletter, youth activities, and anti-drug marches, to less formal activities such as reporting criminal activity and watching neighbors' houses when they are absent. All activities should be determined by the need of the community and neighborhood. Some neighborhoods will need neighborhood clean-ups in order to establish ownership of the neighborhood, while other neighborhoods may have an active association that is able to develop needed youth activities. In all instances the officer must work with community residents and groups to help determine the needs of the community and then assist in developing a plan of action. Different neighborhood groups may have conflicting issues and special interests. If this happens, the officer may have to negotiate with the groups to find common ground. The goal is to have all residents work together to reduce crime and disorder and increase neighborhood safety.

Problem solving is one of the duties assigned to the police officer. The officer and citizens must examine calls for service and problem areas for underlying problems, then work together to solve the problem. This does not mean that arrests and law enforcement are abandoned. Law enforcement is one method of resolving long-term, endemic neighborhood problems. Problem solving should occur in four steps, commonly referred to as the SARA model. These are (1) Scanning, (2) Analyze, (3) Response, and (4) Assessment (Eck & Spelman, 1987). The use of alternative means of problem solving should be encouraged, including civil law, involvement of other agencies, mediation, and education. Whichever solution is chosen, it should be tailored to the problem and to the neighborhood.

By combining positive interaction, partnerships and problem solving, the line officer becomes a beat manager. The beat manager is responsible for knowing about and acting upon issues of public safety, public order and quality of life in neighborhoods. The officer who is a beat manager typically:

- has a college degree,
- is articulate,
- can identify and solve problems,
- is committed to a career as a beat manager,
- is a mediator in conflict resolution situations,
- is capable of conducting investigations,
- is committed to alternatives to arrest,
- but knows how to say, "You're under arrest."

This officer is analytic and possesses problem solving abilities, which separates the beat manager from officers of the past.

Organizational Dimension

The final element of Cordner's community-oriented policing model is the Organizational Dimension. This dimension "surrounds community policing and greatly affects its implementation" (Cordner, 1999). For that reason, many police agencies make changes in their organizational, administrative, management and supervision functions when adopting community-oriented policing. Structure, management and information are some of the elements in the organizational dimension.

Departments have been restructured through decentralization, flattening of the hierarchy, team building, de-specialization and civilianization. Decentralization will allow officers to be closer to the neighborhoods they serve and provide citizens easier access to the police.

Flattening the hierarchy should speed communication, as well as giving officers the authority to make decisions that affect the beat or neighborhood to which they are assigned. The changes in management that generally occur when community-oriented policing is adopted include a new or revised mission statement, strategic planning, mentoring of junior employees by supervisors and other department leaders, empowerment, and selective discipline.

Information has always been a commodity in policing. With the advent of community-oriented policing it is even more important. A police agency will never have sufficient resources to be all things to all people. Information will help police executives, supervisors and officers set priorities based on the most accurate up-to-date information available. Police executives need information to make sure that their goals are being reached and the programs are working (see Chapter One). Officers and supervisors need information in order to perform their enlarged duties. As the line officer becomes a beat manager, the need for accurate up-to-date information is critical. The beat manager needs access to a powerful database that contains information about the assigned beat that can be manipulated to determine problems and problem areas and to implement solutions. Other technology, such as Geographic Information Systems (GIS) can also be used to identify hot-spots. When an agency uses the information it has available to it, in its databases and contact files, identifying problems becomes easier and more cost effective.

Problems Affecting Community-Oriented Policing

The implementation of community-oriented policing is not without problems. As noted earlier in the chapter, agencies have met with resistance when transferring an officer who had been assigned to a neighborhood for a period of time. In some agencies, officers and supervisors have resisted the change to community-oriented policing, challenging a broadened police role. Some see it primarily as a public relations campaign. A frequent misunderstanding is that community-oriented policing means abandoning "tough law enforcement." Studies have revealed higher job satisfaction among officers assigned community-oriented policing duties. However the long-term effect on officers has not been examined (see, for example, Wycoff and Skogan, 1993). Additionally, most studies examined elements of the tactical dimension and have largely ignored the other dimensions (Cordner, 1999). More evaluations of community-oriented policing are needed.

Conclusion

Community-oriented policing is seen by many as a new style of policing, for others it is old wine in a new bottle. However one defines community-oriented policing, it involves not just controlling the bad, but activating the good. This idea represents pro-activism on the part of the police and reinforces social discipline, cooperation and mutual trust between the community and the police while maintaining legal discipline. It requires police executives to activate all possible resources in support of the common good. The four dimensions of Cordner's community policing model can be used as the foundation of a department-wide implementation of community-oriented policing.

Chapter 9

CULTIVATING QUALITY IN POLICING

WITH THE SUCCESS OF TOTAL QUALITY MANAGEMENT in the American manufacturing sector, one would inevitably expect a migration to service industries. And, indeed, by the early 1990s, innumerable service-sector companies were implementing formal quality management programming. Federal Express, for example, has won the Baldrige Award. Transposition to government enterprise was inevitable.

TQM efforts were initiated in innumerable units of the federal bureaucracy during the Bush administration. With the Clinton administration came the "reinventing government" nomenclature, and a continuing commitment to implementing TQM principles in the federal government (Gore 1993). Concurrently, state and local units of government joined the quality management movement. Demands that police agencies do so are inevitable.

But police managers should be very cautious about joining any organizational development movement without carefully examining the applicability of its tenets. In the early 1980s, many units of government tried to implement management by objectives. With few exceptions, the effort failed outright, had nominal impact or fizzled out once the rhetoric wore off. Much of what works well in the manufacturing sector does not translate well to the service sector, either public or private. And what may work in the private service sector may not translate well to government. Caution should be taken regarding the application of TQM to policing. It is intrinsically difficult to quantify quality with regard to the enterprises we relegate to government.

In the private sector, inefficient pension plans are winnowed out. Try proposing elimination of Social Security. One might immediately respond, "That is an unfair comparison." But that is exactly the point. To the extent that government has different objectives, different process rules may also apply. As another example, it makes eminent economic sense for the U.S. Postal Service to eliminate Saturday delivery. But the body politic will not let that happen. Diversity of goals begets inevitable inefficiencies in process. One must be very careful about advocating the American government's wholesale adoption of an organizational development process originally designed to bring Japanese manufacturing to world-class status.

Quality Principles

There are as many lists of TQM principles as there are noteworthy authors on the topic. Sashkin and Kiser (1992) suggest that the principles various TQM consultants and theorists expound can be categorized into three broad premises: culture, customers, and counting. Remembered easily as the three "C's" of TQM, this typology appears to be a useful way to capture the essence of total quality management. Eight phrases describe the elements of TQM culture: measurement for improvement, delegation of decision authority to the lowest possible organizational level, rewards for results, teamwork and cooperation, job security, perceived fairness is reality, equitable rewards, and ownership. The core of TQM is TQM culture. There are three primary elements of customer focus: structured programs to ascertain customer perspective, the internal customer concept, and supplier/provider communication by level of operation personnel. The most complex of the three C's is counting. It consists of more than simply tabulating. There are four elements: specify customers, define supplier specifications, identify steps in work process, and select measurements.

Limitations on Applying TQM Culture to Policing

It is important to carefully consider which TQM elements will translate to a police environment and which will not. Albrecht and Zemke (1985) identified ten characteristics of service-sector enterprises that distinguish them from manufacturing organizations in terms of TQM application. See Table 9.1. Clearly, all of these apply to policing. For example, Albrecht and

Zemke note that service cannot be created in advance and stored in inventory. As an illustration of the problem in law enforcement, we expend a great deal of effort to deploy patrol so officers are reasonably available to citizens on demand.

TABLE 9.1

THE 10 CHARACTERISTICS OF SERVICE

1. Service is produced at the instant of delivery and cannot be created in advance and stored in inventory.

2. Service cannot be centrally produced, inspected, or stockpiled.

3. Service cannot be demonstrated, nor can a sample be sent in advance for approval.

4. In the absence of tangible product, customers value service on the basis of their own personal experience.

5. The service experience cannot be resold or passed on to a third party.

6. Faulty service cannot be recalled.

7. Quality assurance is required before production.

8. Delivery of service usually requires human interactions.

9. Customers' assessments of service quality are subjective and strongly influenced by expectations.

10. Customers' assessments of service quality tend to decrease in proportion to the number of employees they encounter during the delivery of services.

Source: K. Albrecht and R. Zemke, *Service America*

Albrecht and Zemke note that customer assessments of service quality tend to decrease in proportion to the number of employees they encounter during the delivery of services. In a TQM culture, close one-on-one customer/employee relationships are nurtured. Again, developing organizational configurations that allow such relationships is problematic for police agencies. Policing is a 24-hour-a-day operation, and thus different people staff the given positions. Efforts at creating so-called permanent beat assignments are at least partially designed to ameliorate the problem, but they are far from a perfect solution. A customer who calls at 10 a.m. one day and 10 p.m. the next is likely to see a different police officer. Further, the process by which we handle innumerable complaints results in multiple employee contacts with police customers, e.g., referral of long-term investigations from patrol to a detective bureau. Even the manufacturing sector has difficulty in maintaining a single point of contact for customers. But in the service sector and, in particular, in a 24-hour-a-day service endeavor, it is almost impossible. This clearly limits police agencies' ability to apply the "single point of contact" methods TQM consultants suggest.

Interestingly, there are some TQM culture principles that are arguably "overapplied" in policing. One of Deming's 14 points is to "drive out fear." He is referring to fear of eminent job loss. TQM works best when employees have a reasonable sense of job security. The Japanese, of course, have taken this to the extreme of lifetime employment. As Ouchi (1981) noted in *Theory Z*, lifetime employment would never work in the United States. It is possible in Japan only through a compensation system that cuts wages dramatically during corporate difficult times. It also depends on treating large numbers of women as "permanent temporary" workers. In reality, at least until very recently, lifetime employment only applied to males.

So in any case, we have a situation where the American corporate manufacturing sector was urged to provide greater job security to its employees. In particular, corporations were cautioned to "never ever" lay off employees when other employees found more efficient ways to do the job, because suggestions for greater efficiency would stop immediately. When corporate executives visit with groups of police managers, they inevitably note how fortunate police managers are to work in an environment where employees are assured of job security. The reaction among police managers is "you've got to be kidding."

The civil service systems in place in U.S. public safety agencies come as close as any arrangement we have to guaranteed lifetime employment. Motivated by the desire to protect police and fire agencies from partisan political influence, and to prevent police and fire positions from being distributed as political spoils, we have developed one of the most formalized, bureaucratized, rigid, and defined personnel administrative systems in the world. Unless there is gross malfeasance, a police officer, once hired, is quite literally employed for life.

Dismissal for lack of productivity is unheard of. Combine this with a lack of financial inducements to be productive, and it is small wonder that police managers do not see the system as conducive to a commitment to quality. It makes no difference whether an officer has five self-initiated incidents per tour, or five per year, he or she will stay employed and earn the same salary.

The lesson here is that we must be very cautious about the unexamined application of principles from one organizational environment to another.

Limitations on Applying TQM's Customer Focus to Policing

In the private sector, management exhorts employees to *delight* the customer. And certainly, across corporate America, innumerable organizations would love to not merely satisfy but to literally delight the customer. Can the customer focus of total quality management be applied to policing? Unequivocally, the answer is no. Not only *can't* we delight the customer, we don't even *want* to delight the customer. Several elements of this phenomenon merit elaboration.

One's immediate reaction when the issue of customer satisfaction in policing is raised is to think of those whom we arrest and laugh a little. No, we are not going to delight someone we're taking to jail for booking, no matter how well we treat him or her. But to think of the customer in this context is to fail to recognize the problems with applying this concept to police service. People we arrest are customers in only a very narrow sense of the term. They deserve to be treated with dignity and respect, but the police are hardly there to provide them service. Indeed, from one "quality" perspective, they constitute a "defect" that police are eliminating.

The important point is that police agencies are not charged with delighting the average law-abiding citizen, either. Police managers are distributing a scarce government resource, and they are responsible for seeing that the resource is distributed equitably. The average citizen routinely requests, and even demands, more than his or her equitable share of that resource. In residential neighborhoods, everyone wants to see the police drive by more often. Businesses pressure municipal and county governments to provide enhanced police protection. Funeral homes want escort services. Parents want police officers in the schools, both to provide security and to warn children of the dangers of using drugs. The list goes on and on. Further, these are only the very generic demands for police service. Specific cases are even more problematic: the neighborhood complainer who calls the police at the drop of a hat; the eccentric who calls twice a night, every night, to have the police check for strange noises in the attic; merchants who use the police as a substitute for the security service they ought to be providing themselves. Again, the list goes on and on. This leads to a critical point: *Although we may want the police to delight the customer, prudent management of public resources demands that the police leave many customers explicitly unhappy.* If we insist, under the misguided rhetoric of community policing, on delighting the neighborhood complainer, that individual will simply call even more. And, in effect, police managers have misappropriated a precious public resource that should be expended for more important purposes.

Police managers are hardly oblivious to the problem. Using the sanitized terminology *differential response,* agencies across the country have curtailed services. Particularly in urban areas with intense service demands, police managers can no longer afford to send an officer to every request for service. The days when the telephone deployed the patrol force are gone.

Thus, the issue of definition of customer satisfaction for police agencies is far from a simple one. The difficulty arises in trying to give individuals at the level of operations–complaint takers, patrol officers, detectives–reasonable guidelines for responding to the public. While no one expects problematic police customers to be delighted, most administrators don't want them treated with condescending disdain, either. There are countless gray shades of response, depending on the situation. Officers are told, explicitly or implicitly, to exercise discretion and use good judgment. And when a citizen complains, it is not an automatic given that the employee is at fault if the customer is less than delighted. Further, by common experience, police officers know that the job involves dealing with difficult, obstreperous and obnoxious people–not all of whom are offenders. When they receive a lecture consisting of nothing but naive platitudes about how they should be partners with community residents, they are likely to roll their eyes.

Limitations on Applying TQM Counting Techniques

Police have innumerable interactions with citizens where the calibration of quality service is reasonably straightforward. For example, we expect an officer responding to a traffic accident to be courteous (even caring), efficient without being officious, and considerate of what, for the citizen, is a traumatic occurrence. For routine complaints for which the police cannot provide any assistance, we expect officers to tell citizens what other help, if any, is available. And so on.

But there are a lot of citizen encounters for which the measurement of quality interaction is open to considerable debate. For example, the findings from the Minneapolis Domestic Violence Experiment suggest that making arrests in such situations is the best course of action. However, subsequent research has suggested that arrests are not necessarily the best response. And regardless of whether various courses of action will prevent future violence, the quality of officer/disputant interaction in these situations is extraordinarily difficult to specify.

Or take a minor-in-possession case. Are the police to arrest a young person for having a beer to celebrate his or her 21st birthday, when it's 30 minutes before midnight the day before the birthday? How about 24 hours before? How about a week before? Is an officer who writes numerous traffic citations at an "easy pickings" location doing quality police work or not? Is the officer's counter-part on the next shift, who never writes traffic citations at that location because he or she has decided that his or her judgment is better than traffic engineering when it comes to appropriate signage or speed limits-doing quality police work?

The point is a relatively simple one. In the manufacturing sector, defects are relatively simple to identify, and quality is defined fundamentally as a lack of defects. For most of the service sector, quality is a bit more difficult to define, but we could still reach close to a consensus on what a quality interaction is about—think of checking into a hotel or receiving service at a restaurant. Not so in policing. Quality in policing is, first of all, situational. Second, even in a given situation, there are varied perceptions of what a quality transaction is. As the homily goes, for every complex situation there are many who will offer simple solutions, and they're always wrong. So it is with this issue.

The use of simplistic tallies of arrests, citations, field interrogations, and even clearances to measure the adequacy of police performance on both an individual and an agency level is frequently criticized. The criticism is certainly justified. Taken by themselves, these types of measures do not adequately represent how well a police department responds to citizens. (One should note as a caution that some police departments that have attempted to abandon these measures found to their dismay that arrests, citations, and clearances dropped fairly precipitously. It should more accurately be noted that these measures are inadequate in and of themselves, but they are not irrelevant.) More "sophisticated" measures are almost universally seen as desirable.

For example, a police agency might handle an auto theft for which a recovery never occurs or an arrest is never made, but do so in a manner that provides quality service to the victim. First of all, since the loss is a significant one, whether covered by insurance or not, the agency might consider sending an officer out in person to take the report, rather than doing so by "differential response." The officer, in turn, might treat the citizen with compassion and understanding, take time to complete the report, and even commiserate with the citizen for a while about the "sorry state of affairs" when nothing is safe from theft anymore. There could even be a follow-up phone call one week and then one month later to let the citizen know that the report hadn't been forgotten, but nothing had been found. Most of us would agree that the police agency managing the incident in this manner provided quality police service. The vast majority of citizens don't blame the police department when a car is stolen. Indeed, their likely response is "we need more police." Thus, if the police handle an incident well, the victim is likely to be satisfied. But how do you measure this?

About the only practical way is some sort of survey of complainants/victims. "Were you satisfied with the response time? Did the complaint taker treat you courteously? Was the officer at the scene courteous? Did someone contact you to inform you of progress on the case?" And, indeed, numerous police agencies use such surveys. They are probably a good idea, as they provide some feedback regarding quality of service. But they have serious limitations. The same officer can respond to two citizens in exactly the same way regarding exactly the same type of incident, and receive very different ratings. Remember that one of the characteristics of service Albrecht and Zemke postulated was that "customers' assessments of service quality are subjective and strongly influenced by expectations." Some might argue that if one did sufficiently large sampling, errors would cancel themselves out and one would emerge with a reasonable picture of the average quality of service a given officer or agency provided. But conducting surveys is not cheap. The best information is obtained through personal contact, such as a telephone interview, but that's also the most expensive. Even mail surveys get expensive when the sample is large, not only with regard to printing and postage, but also for tabulating data. With the budget constraints typical in the public sector and, arguably, no critical purpose to which such information is to be put, large expenditures for gathering such data are not likely to be sustainable.

Further, this type of information is subject to systematic bias. Officers who are assigned to certain beats at certain times are very likely to receive higher ratings overall than officers assigned to different beats at different times. There is a lot of difference between the people the police talk to at 10 A.M. and those they talk to at 2 A.M.

Another illustration of the difficulty of transferring TQM measures used in the private sector to policing is the reduction of cycle times. This measure is regarded by both the manufacturing and the service sectors as an important indicator of improved quality. Examples abound:

- the check-out time for a rental car,
- the check-in time at a hotel,
- the turnaround time for insurance claims,
- the rapidity of order fulfillment,
- the rapidity of payment cycles, and
- the rapidity with which phones are answered.

Some of these can be applied to policing. For example, we certainly would take rapidity of telephone answering as one measure of quality. Another might be reduction in the amount of time it took a citizen to receive a copy of a traffic accident report. And then there is, of course, the big one—rapidity of response by patrol. But the final illustration represents the dangers in doing a simplistic transfer of typical TQM measures to police service. It is not that response time doesn't make any difference. It often makes a great deal of difference in terms of citizen satisfaction. Although citizens will tolerate delayed response, particularly if the complaint taker informs them that there will be some delay, they will not be happy with inordinately long response delays. In particular, they will not be happy in instances when they are stressed, e.g., waiting in the parking lot of a mall when their car has been stolen. Or let's be more dramatic. Mom, Dad and the kids go to see Grandma and find her dead on the bedroom floor. No family feels like sitting in the living room for two hours, with Grandma on the bedroom floor, waiting for the police to show up. So response time has some import.

Now, let's go back to our earlier scenario on quality handling of an auto theft complaint. In that instance, we dispatched the patrol unit so that our citizen had face-to-face contact with a law enforcement representative to report the very significant loss of property. The officer took his or her time taking the report. And we allocated scarce police resources to a public relations clerk who did routine callbacks. But in doing all that with our scarce police resources, we didn't have officers cruising the streets with uncommitted patrol time, ready to respond rapidly to either the next auto theft complaint or respond to Grandma on the bedroom floor. Which is higher quality police service—taking our time with every complainant, or keeping patrol resources free so that we get to selected complainants more rapidly? There is no answer to this question. Not only is there no unanimity of opinion, but we also aren't even close to a consensus. And, ultimately, no matter which opinion any of us hold, we would have to acknowledge that it's exactly that—an opinion—not a fact.

Not all qualitative elements of police work can be quantified. There are too many exigencies, contingencies, and intangibles. Private-sector consultants who approach a police department with formula solutions to measure quality are purveyors of snake oil. Offering simplistic measurement solutions is *prima facie* evidence of ignorance of the complexity of the police role.

That is not to say that some common TQM measures cannot be applied to police service. Some are relatively easy to tabulate, and some are quite difficult. Some will provide very direct measures of quality, while others will provide only indirect measures. But some measurement is better than none. At the same time, police managers must recognize that we cannot reduce all quality police service to numbers.

Chapter 10

POLITICAL REALITIES

POLICE ADMINISTRATION IS INHERENTLY A POLITICAL PROFESSION. The professional movement in policing, launched by the publication of O.W. Wilson's *Police Administration* in 1950, is often credited with removing politics from policing. It is more accurately stated, however, that the professional movement removed *partisan* politics from policing. The role of a police chief or sheriff is still very much a political one. Most would regard this as perfectly appropriate in any democratic society.

Every police manager is affected by a number of pressure groups in any community. First and foremost, the administrator must deal with the community as a whole. Second, geographic subdivisions of a community are often the focus of special concerns, i.e., neighborhoods. Third, most police managers must give special attention to the chamber of commerce and business groups. Fourth, the service clubs and related community action groups merit special attention. These groups are usually not the locus of negative pressure. However, they can be instrumental in garnering support for development and changes in an agency. Finally, every community has a set of special interest groups. They range from abuse shelters to senior citizen groups.

Interaction With the Community As a Whole

Successful police managers employ a variety of means to communicate with the community as a whole. Attendance at community meetings is essential. As the chief executive officer of the police organization, it is expected that a police chief or sheriff will attend a number of these meetings himself/herself. Some things in a police agency cannot be delegated, and this is one. That is not to say that an assistant chief or captain cannot attend some meetings in lieu of the chief or sheriff. However, if a police chief or sheriff almost never attends any community meetings, it will be noted.

The saying "can't see the forest for the trees" truly applies when trying to assess the agency image in the community. Community perception of the operation of the department remains critical. An individual agency and chief executive may be held in high regard by the law enforcement community. Fraternal groups and associations may praise the chief who has guided and led that agency to a successful transition to community policing. But these praises without similar accolades from the community will only be additional references in an updated resumè.

One department's image suffered because of the public's belief that steps were not being taken to address increased gang activity in the community. In fact, substantial steps had been taken to address increased gang activity, including the assignment of officers to gather and process gang intelligence, target identification and acquisition, and arrests of targeted individuals. These actions were completed in cooperation with the state's attorney's office. This combined effort and action plan had a significant impact on local gang organizers. But because the department had kept success strictly an internal matter, the public thought nothing had been done to resolve the gang problem.

Interaction with news media is, to say the least, an integral part of interacting with the community as a whole. Like it or not, a great deal of public perception of the police is molded by the news media. There is certainly a time for "no comment." However, the vast majority of time a police manager is expected to provide feedback to the news media. It is easy to become angry about perceived unfair reporting or sensationalist coverage. Failure to provide feedback to news media premised upon such anger, however, inevitably backfires.

Media Relations Guidelines

1. If the media can obtain information through the Freedom of Information Act, give the media the information. Don't unnecessarily put the media through difficult procedures.
2. It has been the experience of many police chiefs and sheriffs that when the media is refused information, the issue then turns into a "big story." They will develop their own resources, obtaining the information anyway. The story is not likely to be flattering to the police agency.
3. Make sure that all of the information is accurate. There have been many occasions in which, after he/she has received information from a third or fourth source and has given it to reporters, a police chief has learned that it was inaccurate. This undermines confidence.
4. A police chief or sheriff should schedule a press conference whenever a major crime or disaster has occurred. When the community is upset about circumstances and events surrounding a situation, the police chief or sheriff herself/himself must give the press conference. Utilizing a public information officer is an excellent way to provide information on the daily activities of the police department; however, when a major event takes place, the police chief or sheriff must be the one who presents that information.
5. Use the media to get important information to the public. A police chief or sheriff should have regular meetings with the media to make better use of this conduit.
6. Know the media's deadlines. Each media outlet may have a different deadline. It is important to learn their deadlines in order to get back to a reporter in a timely manner. They will appreciate the consideration, and be more responsive to the chief's thoughts, ideas and quotes.
7. The media should be viewed as an animal "that must be fed when it is hungry because, if you don't feed it, it will eat you."
8. Don't get angry at rookie reporters. Instead, help them learn how to conduct an interview and write a story. Time spent with a reporter should not be considered a waste of time.
9. It is important for both the media and the police to learn each other's roles, expectations, and goals. It is very important to remember that the media is in the entertainment industry, a for-profit business.
10. Both the public information officer and the media should know the "rules of the game." Chiefs and sheriffs need to remember that any off-the-record comment will typically be "on the record." Just avoid the practice.

Successful police managers monitor the pulse of a community by using several sources. The tone of correspondence to the police department should be monitored. The nature and frequency of formal complaints should be known to a police chief or sheriff. Letters to the editor are frequently written by chronic complainers, but their overall tone is an indication of community perception of the police department.

More formally, some police agencies have even employed structured surveys to obtain feedback regarding a community's perception of police effectiveness. Often such surveys can be distributed as part of utility billing mailings. Surveys are sometimes helpful in identifying trends that may be damaging department credibility or actual misconduct by an officer or group of officers. They are expensive to administer and should be carefully developed so that meaningful analysis can be made of the results. Many police managers are apprehensive about conducting this type of survey, as negative feedback may be used politically against the administrator or department. However, the benefits of conducting these surveys outweighs the negatives, and citizens appreciate the opportunity to comment/vent about police services. Random samples are best. Survey results should be available to members of the department and the community through the media.

There are four general categories of questions that may be considered:

1. Source characteristics
2. Opinions regarding various police services
3. Opinions regarding criminal activities
4. Attitude toward police

The use of the classic police report writing tool may be helpful: who, what, when, where and why. The "who" portion addresses the individuals that the department wants to survey. The manner in which the source group is contacted will determine the source group. A mass mailing, random telephone/mail survey of an entire service population, or a specific portion of the service population may be targeted. A section requesting some general demographic information is generally included containing questions regarding:

1. Years lived in community
2. Community type (urban-rural-village-city)
3. Age-Race-Sex

4. Annual income
5. Educational background
6. Employment status

The "what" portion (what does the agency want to know) affects the source selection. A general survey to seek community perception of crime may best be pursued with a mass mailing to the entire community. Such mailings are generally anonymous and may include questions regarding:

1. How serious does the respondent view crime in the community?
2. Has the crime problem become better or worse over a particular period of time?

The following questions tailor the survey to more specific crime and police services issues:

1. What contact have you had with a police officer during the past year?
2. How do you rate the quality of police services?
3. Do you think the police do a satisfactory job of investigating crimes?
4. Should officers be required to maintain a mandatory level of physical fitness and appearance based on age and sex?

The "when" portion may relate to a general time frame in which a concern was noted such as: "During the last year has concern about crime made you anxious when you were walking/cycling, alone at home, at work or anywhere at night?" Similarly, a question may be formed regarding improving and/or deteriorating conditions over a one, five or ten-year period.

The "where" portion may address the community itself or a specific section within the community. The survey must clearly specify the area in question. Finally, the surveying agency must clearly identify "why" the survey is being pursued.

In addition to simply monitoring the tone of community satisfaction, proactive efforts should be implemented to convey the police agency perspective. Some of these are discussed in the chapter on community policing. Agencies have gone so far as to develop a police program for local access cable television. Many agencies send representatives to participate on talk radio programs. Others employ formal focus groups drawn from segments of the community of particular concern. Some police managers maintain a community leader list and routinely check in with these individuals. The internet has become a new medium of communication. One should also remember that citizens who have formal interaction with the police department–volunteers, citizen police academies, neighborhood watches, citizen on patrol groups–are a source of feedback regarding community perceptions.

Neighborhood Groups

Every neighborhood wants special attention from the police. One of the balancing acts that a police manager must perform is responsiveness to vociferous neighborhood associations against service to neighborhoods in need of attention, but less politically demanding. In particular, neighborhoods housing transients, such as apartment complexes, require attention. It is easy to focus all additional resources available in an agency on neighborhoods where associations appear at city council meetings, to the detriment of "wheels that are not quite as squeaky." A police manager should also be careful not to assume that a neighborhood association is representative of the neighborhood as a whole. Some certainly are, and represent legitimate cross-sectional concerns. Others, however, are held captive by a few individuals whose concerns may not reflect those of the entire neighborhood.

Caution When Commenting on Crime Issues

A police chief may attempt to downplay certain issues and be successful in convincing the community that the fears are not valid. But if a critical incident occurs, a chief can be placed in an embarrassing position, forced to restate his original position based on some after-the-fact event.

An example is gang influence in small and medium-sized communities. Total denial may reduce fear of gangs and raise the comfort level of the community. But when evidence of gang activity emerges, the chief may regret those previous words of comfort.

Neighborhood associations should not be regarded, however, as merely problematic pressure groups. They represent enormous opportunity for cooperative community endeavors. The merger of block watch programs, or citizen on patrol programs, with structured neighborhood associations should certainly be considered. Beat officers may be assigned responsibility for intensive liaison with neighborhood associations. Illustrations of productive working relationships between police agencies and neighborhood associations abound.

Chamber and Business Groups

Business groups in most communities are likely to be highly influential. Members of the business community disproportionately hold public office. They are typically the genesis of community development efforts. They also demand police service.

Again, the role of the police manager is to assure that balance is struck between the interest of business groups and the community as a whole. Assigning a foot patrol officer to a business sector may be a good idea and will certainly be supported by relevant business groups. Resources required for such an assignment must be weighed against other demands on a police department. There are no formulas that will provide an answer to a police manager regarding the appropriate balance to be struck. If a police manager must say 'no' to business groups, then the reason for the negative response should be made clear, e.g., "I have to make a choice between a D.A.R.E. program in our middle school or a foot patrol officer downtown." It must also be remembered that assigning additional patrol to commercial areas is not necessarily pandering to business groups. The general public is appreciative of the additional security and service that such assignments provide. The problem is deciding what is legitimate expenditure of public funds, and when the line is crossed that constitutes provision of private security services.

Service Clubs

Service clubs are still an important part of the political life of most communities, particularly smaller ones. The police manager must first decide whether to join one or more service clubs. Again, there is no prescription in this respect–appropriate judgment will vary from community to community and in terms of the proclivities of individual police managers. Police managers should certainly be prepared to routinely make presentations to service clubs. They are in this sense part of the manager's obligation to attend community meetings.

Special Interest Groups

Numerous special interest groups have concern with police policy and programs. Police managers need to be careful not to (1) psychologically group all special interests together, and (2) regard any special interest group as simply a thorn in the side. Special interest groups certainly include extremists. And the demands of some special interest groups are certainly unreasonable. Further, most police managers are likely to politically disagree with special interest groups more often than they will agree with them. But most social and political change in a democracy is at least accelerated by special interest groups. The law enforcement community is, from one perspective, a special interest group itself. So, once again it is balance in perspective that is important. Special interest groups merit the attention of police managers, but police managers must be careful that they do not consume all of her/his discretionary time.

Citizen Complaints

The internal affairs' function is the "Achilles' heel" of any police chief and has the most potential for volatile influence upon the chief's career. A well-written internal affairs policy, accompanied by a manual of rules and regulations and general orders, is essential to success. Responsiveness and a positive effort to resolve complaints about police service/conduct are an important function of the organization. Citizens' complaints should be resolved through a formal process. Some departments publish a printed pamphlet that outlines the complaint process.

Elected Officials

One of the biggest frustrations a police chief or sheriff can experience is elected officials, believing they are experts on law enforcement, attempting to micro-manage the department. The other side of the coin is that many times a chief will not accept even general direction or a broad agenda set forth by an elected political body. In either case, the result will be frustration. A chief of police should not allow elected officials to manage the department. Responsible public officials do not attempt to do so. But elected officials should set a broad agenda.

The police chief or sheriff must establish an ongoing business relationship with members of a city council or county board. He/she should provide them with information about a broad range of issues in the community, including crime, trends in criminal behavior, traffic, youth and gang problems, and police agency involvement in quality of life efforts. The key is to communicate, communicate, communicate. By routinely talking to all elected officials, whether a chief or sheriff likes them personally or not, police effectiveness will be increased. Additionally, a chief should remember that it is harder to fire someone that you know well than someone that you don't. Beyond simply knowing a chief well, if a city council feels their police chief is a law enforcement expert who has compassion, understanding, and listens closely to their needs, as well as being a problem solver, the chief will have a longer tenure.

Newly elected political officials merit special attention. As a police manager, one must remember that it is "all new to them." Time should be taken to explain department programs and policy, and provide a historical perspective on those programs and policies. It is wise to ascertain informally what the newly elected official's prior experiences with law enforcement have been. Previous negative experiences with law enforcement do not necessarily portend a disastrous relationship. Some of the strongest supporters of organizations are individuals who have had previous negative experiences with similar entities, and perceive the police manager as an administrator trying to change things for the better.

The ongoing debate regarding the purpose and role of government in our society has surfaced in the council chambers and mayoral offices of many local governments. Debate rages over whether governments and police departments should expand or reduce services. Conservatives push for the reduction or even elimination of services and departments, while liberals seek expanded services and roles. As these forces ebb and flow within a community, the functions and roles of a police department that were supported yesterday can quickly become anathema today. A police chief or sheriff must stay constantly politically attuned.

Political Statesmanship

- A chief should refrain from upstaging politicians. For example, if an alderman or any other elected official comes up with a good idea, even if the chief had a similar idea, the elected official should be given credit. Indeed, truly adept police chiefs will make their idea that of elected officials.

- Politicians, like other human beings, will become defensive if they are embarrassed, especially in public. An elected official may seek revenge or simply may not support any of the police chief's ideas or requests, no matter how legitimate they might be. Many chiefs have lost jobs after embarrassing politicians. And those that kept their jobs may not have gotten needed resources for their police departments.

- Police managers should avoid battles over resources in the political arena. The police must clearly state their objectives and their needs by using clear and concise facts, not emotion. After the chief clearly communicates the needs of the department including the rationale for requests, it is out of the chief's hands. Chiefs who find it necessary to "win all of the battles" typically lose the war. A chief should not get emotionally involved in budget requests. Another budget cycle will come.

- Police managers should beware of social events favoring one political person over another. If a chief is invited to attend a gathering of elected officials, he/she should be sure it is non-partisan.

- When attempting to shape public opinion or garner public support, sensitivity to elected officials is essential. We all know that the public is concerned about crime. Recent polls conducted by political candidates throughout the country in municipal, county, state, and federal elections underscore that crime is a top concern. A police chief or sheriff should not misinterpret that concern, however, as a blank check for expanded programming. Elected officials must balance the budget among numerous competing causes.

It may seem pedantic, but the first question a police manager needs to ask is "What is it that I want from elected officials?" A budget is usually the first thing that comes to mind. However, a police manager doesn't merely want "a budget," but specific budgetary modifications. If the budget is going to be supportive of program initiatives in the police agency, then the support of elected political officials is essential. One must learn what their agendas are. One must ascertain what their perceptions of the police department are. And obviously they must be sold on the need for modifications in police programming.

The form of government will establish many of the rules for the game in dealing with elected officials. A local government with a strong mayor will require different interaction than that with a strong city manager. Single-member council or commission districts beget different problems than at-large districts. Charter requirements will sometimes place parameters around political interaction. There are, finally, individual proclivities, political ideologies and typically a local political culture that have evolved over decades that place some additional parameters on how public administrators deal with elected officials. A police chief or sheriff new to the role should be very careful to ascertain what the expectations of the local political culture are. Deviation from that culture should be done with great caution.

Different types of local government structure may dictate different reporting methods. Many chiefs, for example, are required to report directly to a city manager, while others answer only to a mayor or commissioner. Sometimes public safety commissioners are elected at-large within a community and actually have administrative and operational authority over the chief of police and the chief's subordinates.

An American law enforcement agency is an institution of democracy. Our democracy is the product of compromise. Our Constitution and, in particular, the Bill of Rights are the result of compromise. Had that compromise failed, the United States of America would not exist as we know it today. The kind of compromise that we witnessed over two hundred years ago is a political process. Nonetheless, too many police managers speak of all political compromise as a tarnished process. They refer disparagingly to politicians when they are forced by our political system to adjust their positions on important issues. They accuse politicians of "selling out" if they settle on a position different than that upon which a campaign was based. But they also complain when a politician's stubbornness results in government "gridlock."

Constitutional provisions, both state and national, prevent law enforcement from operating independent of scrutiny. That scrutiny comes from all three branches of government–the executive, legislative and judicial. Any police administrator who fails to accept the reality of, and need for, such scrutiny is destined for a difficult career at best. Democracy, as a governmental system, includes mistrust of law enforcement. Concentrated authority is alien to democratic principles. In the United States the public is willing to accept the high costs of separate, but overlapping police jurisdictions to ensure decentralization of authority. Police managers should never underestimate how inherently strong a "healthy mistrust" of the police is in our governmental system.

But It Was Community Policing....

Recently a highly successful police chief in southern Illinois faced a challenge from newly elected members of his city council over the fact that his department participated in programs such as D.A.R.E., school liaison, and other youth oriented initiatives. In one instance a councilman stated that he had observed a police officer helping a child fix a flat tire on her bike, and he felt that this was the kind of activity that police officers should not be doing. The amazed and somewhat stunned police chief asked why this was a problem. The councilman's response was that police officers reaching out to children in this and other ways were examples of government attempting to take over the role of parents.

Elections of aldermen, trustees, commissioners, mayors and board members frequently engender debate about the issues of public safety and crime. Police chiefs are "political animals," despite the fact that the position is appointed. A sheriff's position is inherently political. But the independent elected nature of the office does not absolve a sheriff from an obligation of cooperative political interaction. The sheriff has to be considerate of the political needs of those county board members who adopt operational budgets and approve staffing needs. In some cases there are partisan political issues that must be set aside.

> **Priorities**
>
> A new police chief was applying for a position in a small resort community. During the interview, the elected officials advised the applicant that their biggest concern was people walking their dogs on the beach. Those dogs, in turn, would leave feces, which wouldn't be removed by the owners. They said that other than that concern, they felt they had a good community. They wanted to keep it quiet, with limited controversy. The applicant said he understood and thought he could do a good job for the community. After being hired, the chief studied all the problems within the community and found a few serious ones.
>
> First, the main route through town had been the site of numerous fatal accidents for years. To remedy the situation, he trained his officers in traffic enforcement, purchased a radar unit and began writing traffic tickets. Accidents were significantly reduced and there were no fatalities on that route during his first year.
>
> Second, the chief noted that there had been a series of burglaries in the condominium complexes. The chief and his staff developed a surveillance plan. The plan worked, and offenders were subsequently arrested. As it turned out, these offenders were responsible for almost all the burglaries in the complexes. The arrests occurred during the first month of the chief's tenure, resulting in a drastic reduction in total burglaries in that small resort community.
>
> The chief was very proud of himself. He realized that he dramatically cut down on both the accident and the burglary rates. However, the chief was in for a surprise when he went to the city council meeting where they were deciding his reappointment. The mayor told him that he would not be reappointed. Incredulously, the chief recounted how he had reduced both the burglary and the accident fatality rates in the past year. The mayor and the council members looked at each other, and said that he had done a great job in that respect. However, the reason he wasn't being reappointed was because he had not addressed the main concern of the community—the walking of dogs on the beach. He had forgotten one important lesson—elected officials are the representatives of the people, and have a right to set priorities for the police department.

Regardless of the governmental structure, it is very important that the elected officials be kept appropriately informed. Generally, city council or county board committee meetings are a proper forum for the exchange of information. City council members have an obligation to correct problems brought to their attention. Although infrastructure needs often consume their time, an alderman will often receive complaints about police matters like traffic violations and the fear of crime. The wise law enforcement administrator will respect the elected official's obligation and address the problem with sincerity and a commitment to a subsequent status report.

Caution must always be exercised so that interaction does not become interference. Usually interference is the product of enthusiasm rather than corruption. It is a manifestation of a desire to be better informed and feel more included. The situation should be handled delicately–but handled. A luncheon meeting or private conference may provide individuals tending to cross the line with insight without compromising an important investigation or prosecution.

City Manager

The police chief and the city manager must establish mutual understanding. For the police chief, the city manager can be either the most trusted ally or the most feared enemy. Additionally, it is important to know that both the police chief and the city manager have the most sensitive of municipal positions. In order for the chief to work well with the manager, he/she must keep the city manager informed at all times. It is very embarrassing for the city manager to receive calls from elected officials about a serious police problem about which he/she has never been informed. If the city manager has to start calling for information from the police department when a serious incident has occurred, the next step will be the city manager's attempt to manage the police department.

One should debate with the city manager in private . A police chief should never embarrass the city manager in front of elected officials. For example, if the city manager cuts a number of positions out of the budget and a police chief is asked by the city council why she/he is not asking for those positions, she/he should dispassionately review the process–deferring to the city manager at an appropriate time.

An astute police chief also uses the city manager as a political buffer. If aldermen or trustees contact the police chief with a request, the police chief should appropriately handle the request, then report to the city manager with the solution or answer for the aldermen. The city manager can then call the alderman with the answer. In that way, the response conditions the elected officials to contact the city manager instead of the police chief. However, some city managers prefer that the police chief contact the elected official with the necessary information, simply advising the manager of what transpired.

Mistakes should be openly acknowledged with the city manager. The best policy is to admit the mistake, explain why it happened and what will be done to rectify the problem. It is important to live up to mistakes. It will help to instill trust between a police chief and a city manager.

There are times when a city manager may make requests that a police chief feels are inappropriate. It is up to the police chief to explain discreetly to the manager why it is inappropriate. Conversely, city managers do not support police chiefs who, every time a request is made, finds reasons why it can't be fulfilled. Managers are looking for problem solvers.

Other City/County Departments

A police agency should not be an island in city/county government. Many of the recent community policing initiatives have involved the development of cooperative relationships with other city/county departments. It is extremely unusual, however, for other city/county departments to initiate cooperative efforts with their police department. It falls upon the shoulders of law enforcement managers to first reach out to other department heads. The nature of police work is such that other department officials tend to avoid getting too close to the law enforcement agency for fear that they will be perceived as prying. Unfortunately, this reluctance has prevented cooperative radio uses, joint purchasing, logical traffic control recommendations, and many other coordinated efforts toward better government.

Traditionally, competition exists among department heads. If a police department gets new equipment and a fire department doesn't, or if compensation is perceived to be inequitable among departments, then friction may develop among the department heads. This is especially prevalent at budget time. Those governments that are considered most responsive to their citizens require department heads to work closely together.

SCHOOLS. During the last decade police agencies have become

increasingly involved with schools. The occasional lecture on bicycle safety 40 years ago has evolved to full-time school assignments for large numbers of sworn personnel. School resource officer programs, D.A.R.E. programs, G.R.E.A.T. programs, and other school liaison efforts now consume a fair proportion of police resources. The assignment of officers to full-time roles in schools often creates problematic supervision problems. Further, while some schools welcome the police with open arms, others accept their presence only grudgingly. A balance between prevention and communication efforts with enforcement endeavors must be struck. Efforts must be made to delineate distinctions between school discipline issues and delinquency issues. And even with the best effort, there will be a gray zone.

FIRE. Productive relationships with fire/EMS departments are also a part of a police manager's role. There are often facility use issues, safety education coordination, and code and building inspection coordination that must be articulated. Again, a solid working relationship can lead to considerably enhanced public safety.

SANITATION. Sanitation departments are frequently overlooked by police managers as a source of cooperative support. Professional sanitation departments can assist departments in identifying problem locations. They should be a core part of community policing efforts to improve the quality of life in neighborhoods. Many agencies have cooperative arrangements on vacant lot cleanups, for example. Sanitation departments are also involved in some communities in graffiti control.

OTHER DEPARTMENTS. Liaison with other city/county departments will also require the time of a police manager. The linkage to traffic engineering is evident. Cooperative efforts with parks and recreation departments are often a part of neighborhood improvement programs in which the police department participates. Some police agencies have become intimately involved with public housing agencies, placing mini police stations in public housing developments. There is literally no other city/county department with which the police at some point and time do not have contact.

CRIMINAL JUSTICE AGENCIES. Part of the politics of policing is the management of relationships with other criminal justice agencies. Obviously, relationships with other police departments often become highly politicized. The public is understandably not very tolerant of rivalries among agencies that degenerate to infighting. Maintaining solid relations with the state's attorney, public defenders/defense attorneys, court administrators, judges, jail administrators, probation officers, and parole officers is a constant challenge. Even maintaining cooperation among police agencies can be problematic. Relationships between local agencies and the state police have the potential for misunderstandings. Police managers should expect disagreements with individuals in these roles. The criminal justice system is deliberately designed so that it does not become one big happy family. To the extent possible, police chiefs and sheriffs should strive to maintain the natural stress among these relationships as part of the ongoing process of professional public administration. When political vendettas occur, 99 percent of the time everyone loses.

Working with federal agencies is not as difficult as one might be led to believe. Shared information without restrictions will never be achieved. However, federal authorities have the same general goals and are often willing to cooperate despite their reputations. Cooperative reluctance is sometimes caused by a failure of local chiefs and sheriffs to include federal authorities in professional and social events. Cooperative measures need not be complex joint case investigations. An agreement to jointly present a security program to bankers, or a mail fraud seminar to senior citizens, will establish relationships.

A Sheriff's Political Role

There is generally a great deal of pressure on sheriff candidates to make campaign promises. Sheriff candidates too easily can let promises made become promises broken. Great care and thought should be taken in making promises. If it is necessary to make promises, they should be kept simple and doable. A sheriff candidate should restrain the urge to promise too much. Some promises will require the cooperation of others—can this cooperation be obtained? If so, at what price? If campaign promises cannot be kept, the issue should be faced head-on. An honest presentation of the issue can bring positive results by demonstrating basic openness and honesty.

As an elected law enforcement executive, there are numerous other elected officials whose functions relate to the duties of the sheriff's. Common goals require cooperation and communication. Frequently, however, members of the sheriff's same political party will cause the biggest headaches. Political backers are necessary. Most are good, honest people and are not looking for special favors. They are, in fact, looking for someone who is fair and honest. But inevitably some believe that party affiliation gives them special status. Favors may be sought, and in extreme instances political allies may seek exception to the law. If ever there is quicksand along the path to being a good sheriff, this is it. Ethical positions and values must be upheld.

When running for office, one of the most difficult issues is what political support should be expected from the employees of the sheriff's office. There are no easy answers to this question. Should monetary contributions be accepted? What about officers distributing literature? In some states, election laws give candidates guidelines. The final answer must rest with the individual and his/her own set of values.

Influencing Legislation

Changes in labor laws and changes in the criminal code are among many factors that, through legislation, will affect the way a chief or sheriff approaches organizational and community problems. Therefore, it is essential that an administrator interact with legislators regarding pending bills or proposals through personal contact and correspondence. However, a chief or sheriff is usually wise to avoid taking positions that are essentially unrelated to the needs of the profession. It is even wise to withhold public comment on the merits of important issues that may have some indirect impact on law enforcement. A bond issue for a new school, for example, may preclude a tax increase for a new jail. Nevertheless, it does not serve the chief or sheriff to become embroiled in avoidable controversy.

On the other hand, local issues with direct impact are sometimes of such importance that the administrator's view should be public. Proposals to increase speed limits, legalize illicit drugs or authorize use of certain weapons are examples of subjects that merit public comment from those in law enforcement who understand the consequences of legislative passage or rejection. These are sometimes partisan issues. The key is to take a stand without presenting oneself as a spokesperson for a given party or a group outside law enforcement.

Occasionally, an issue unique to the locality will require the attention of an administrator. It may be as basic as permitted "trick-or-treat" days, or as complex as the financing of a new facility. Such issues affect operations, and most citizens expect and deserve comment from their law enforcement leaders.

Almost all police chiefs and sheriffs belong to professional organizations that closely follow legislative proposals and developments. These associations and, in some instances, alliances are critical. They can exist without law enforcement as a profession becoming submerged in distasteful political bickering. The associations also help as a resource providing information, political lobby, and technical assistance.

BIBLIOGRAPHY

Albrecht, K., and Zemke, R. (1985). *Service America.* Homewood, IL.: Dow Jones–Irwin.

Asner, M. (1998). "A fair fight: Government resellers deserve open competition and complaint resolution." *Government Technology Reseller;* September, 1998; pages 18 & 19.

ASQC Quality Costs Committee. (1987). *Guide for Reducing Quality Costs.* Milwaukee: ASQC Quality Press.

Bittner, E. (1990). *Aspects of Police Work.* Boston: Northeastern University Press.

Bloch, P. & Bell, J. (1976). *Managing Criminal Investigations: The Rochester System.* Washington, DC: The Police Foundation.

Bolman, L. G. and Deal, T. E. (1997). Second Edition. *Reframing Organizations.* San Francisco: Jossey–Bass.

Bopp, William and Whisenand, Paul. (1980). *Police Personnel Administration* (2nd Ed.). Boston: Allyn and Bacon.

Boydstun, J.E. (1975). *San Diego Field Interrogation: Final Report.* Washington, DC: The Police Foundation.

Braiden, C. R. (1992). "Enriching Traditional Roles." In L. Hoover (ed.) *Police Management Perspectives and Issues.* Washington, DC: Police Executive Research Forum.

Brocka, B., and Brocka, S.M. (1992). *Quality Management: Implementing the Best Ideas of the Masters.* Homewood, IL.: Business One Irwin.

Center for Disease Control. (1997). "Ten Leading Causes of Death in the U. S." *Monthly Vital Statistics Report,* Volume 46, No. 1 Supplement.

Couper, D.C., and. Lobitz, S.H (1991). *Quality Policing: The Madison Experience.* Washington, DC.: Police Executive Research Forum.

Cordner, Gary W. (1992). "Human Resource Issues." In Hoover, L. T. (ed.) *Police Management Perspectives & Issues.* Washington, DC: Police Executive Research Forum.

Cordner, G.W. & Trojanowicz, R.C. (1992). "Patrol." In G.W. Cordner & D.C. Hale (Eds.), *What Works in Policing.* Cincinnati: Anderson Publishing Co.

Cordner, Gary W. (1999). "Elements of Community Policing." In Gaines, L. K. and Cordner, G. W. *Policing Perspectives.* Los Angeles, CA: Roxbury Publishers.

Crosby, P.B. (1979). *Quality is Free.* New York: McGraw-Hill.

Crosby, P.B. (1984). *Quality Without Tears.* New York: McGraw-Hill.

del Carmen, R. V. (1998). *Criminal Procedure: Law and Practice* (4th Edition), Belmont, CA.: Wadsworth Publishing Company.

Delattre, E. J. (1996). *Character and Cops: Ethics in Policing.* Washington, DC: AEI Press.

Delattre, E. J. (1991). *Against Brutality and Corruption: Integrity, Wisdom, and Professionalism.* Tallahassee, FL: Florida Criminal Justice Executive Institute.

Deming, W.E. (1986). *Out of the Crisis.* Cambridge, MA.: MIT Center for Advanced Engineering Study.

Department of Commerce. (1995). *Malcolm Baldrige National Quality Award,* 1995 *Award Criteria.* Washington, DC.: Government Printing Office.

Dobyns, L., and Crawford-Mason, C. (1991). *Quality OR ELSE: The Revolution in World Business.* Boston: Houghton Mifflin.

Eck, J.E. (1983). *Solving Crimes. The Investigation of Burglary and Robbery.* Washington, DC: Police Executive Research Forum.

Eck, J.E. (1992). "Criminal Investigations." In G.W. Cordner & D.C. Hale (Eds.), *What Works in Policing.* Cincinnati: Anderson Publishing Co.

Eck, J.E. & Spelman, W. (1987). *Problem-Solving: Problem-Oriented Policing in Newport News.* Washington, DC: Police Executive Research Forum.

Ernst & Young Quality Improvement Consulting (Group). (1990). *Total Quality: An Executives Guide for the 1990s.* Homewood, IL.: Business One Irwin.

Federal Bureau of Investigation. (1991). *Crime in the United States [Uniform Crime Reports].* Washington, DC: U.S. Government Printing Office.

Froemel, Ernest C. (1979). "Objective and Subjective Measure of Police Officer Performance." In Spielberger, Charles D. (ed.) *Police Selection and Evaluation: Issues and Techniques.* New York: Praeger.

Gale,. B., and Buzzell, R. (1987). *The PIMS Principles: Linking Strategy to Performance.* New York: Free Press.

Garvin, D.A. (1988). *Managing Quality.* New York: Free Press.

Goldstein, H. (1975). *Police Corruption: A Perspective on its Nature and Control.* Washington, DC: Police Foundation.

Goldstein, H. (1977). *Policing a Free Society.* Cambridge, MA: Ballinger Publishing.

Gore, A. (1993). *The Gore Report on Reinventing Government.* New York: Random House.

Grant, E.L., and Leavenworth, R.S. (1980). *Statistical Quality Control.* New York: McGraw-Hill.

Greenwood, P. & Petersilia, J. (1975). *The Criminal Investigation Process. Volume I: Summary and Policy Implications.* Santa Monica, CA: RAND Corporation.

Grimm, A.F. (ed.). (1986). *Quality Costs.* Milwaukee: ASQC Quality Press.

Hagan, J.T. (ed.). (1984). *Principles of Quality Costs.* Milwaukee: ASQC Quality Press.

Hanna, D. (1990). *Police Executive Leadership.* Champaign, IL.: Stipes Publishing Co.

Hatry, H.P., and Greiner, J.M. (1986). *Improving the Use of Quality Circles in Police Departments.* Washington, DC.: National Institute of Justice.

Hawk, D. (1994). *Total Quality Management:* Fact or Fantasy. Houston: Champion Press.

Herzberg, F. (1966). *Work and the Nature of Man.* Cleveland: World.

Hoover, L.T. (1996). *Quantifying Quality in Policing.* Washington, DC.: Police Foundation.

Imai, M. (1986). *Kaizen: The Key to Japans Competitive Success*. New York: Random House Business Division.

Ishikawa, K. (1985). *What is Total Quality Control? The Japanese Way*. Translated by David J. Lu. Englewood Cliffs, N.J.: Prentice-Hall.

Jones, Tony L. (1998). "Developing Performance Standards." *Law and Order,* July, pages 109-112.

Juran, J.M. (1988). *Juran on Planning for Quality*. New York: Free Press.

Kansas City, Mo., Police Department. (1977). *Response Time Analysis*. Washington, DC.: U.S. Department of Justice, National Institute of Law Enforcement and Criminal Justice.

Kelling, G.L., Pate, T., Dieckman, D., & Brown, C.E. (1974). *The Kansas City Preventive Patrol Experiment: A Technical Report*. Washington, DC: The Police Foundation.

Koby, T.G. & Lucy, V.M. (1992). "Two Promising Concepts in Trouble." *Law Enforcement News*, XVIII, 352 (February 14, 1992).

Lawler, E.E. (1986). *High-Involvement Management*. Washington, DC.: Jossey-Bass.

Lindbloom, C. E. (1959). "The Science of Muddling Through." *Public Administration Review*, Vol. 19, No. 2. Spring, 1959.

March, J. & Simon, H. (1958). *Organizations*. New York: John Wiley.

McCarthy, W. (1977). "A Police Administrator Looks at Police Corruption." *Criminal Justice Center Monograph Number 5*. New York City: John Jay College of Criminal Justice.

Martinson, R. (1974). "What Works? Questions and Answers About Prison Reform." *Public Interest*, 35, 22-54.

McGregor, D. (1960). *The Human Side of Enterprise*. New York: McGraw-Hill.

Miller, L.M. (1984). *American Spirit: Visions of a New Corporate Culture*. William Morrow & Co. Inc.

Millward, R.E. (1968). "PPBS: Problems of Implementation." *American Institute of Planners Journal*. Vol. 34:2, p. 90.

Mintzberg, H. (1989). *Mintzberg on Management: Inside Our Strange World of Organizations*. New York: The Free Press.

Morgan, B. (1981). *Managing Communications for Productivity: Interpersonal Relations*. Munice, IN: Accelerated Development, Inc.

Moore, M.H. & Stephens, D.W. (1991). *Beyond Command and Control: The Strategic Management of Police Departments*. Washington, DC: Police Executive Research Forum.

Oncken, W. (1984). *Managing Management Time: Whos Got the Monkey?* Englewood Cliffs, NJ.: Prentice-Hall.

Ott, S. J. (1996). *Classic Readings in Organizational Behavior*. Second Edition. Belmont, CA: Wadsworth.

Ouchi, W.G. (1981). *Theory Z*. Reading, MA.: Addison-Wesley.

Pate, T., Ferrara, A., Bowers, R., & Lorence, J. (1976). *Police Response Time: Its Determinants and Effects*. Washington, DC: The Police Foundation.

Peters, T.J., and Waterman, R.H. (1982). *In Search of Excellence*. New York: Harper & Row.

Peters, T.J., and Austin, N. (1985). *A Passion for Excellence: The Leadership Difference.* New York: Random House.

Pollock, J. M. (1994). *Ethics in Crime and Justice: Dilemmas and Decisions* (2nd ed.). Belmont, CA: Wadsworth.

Presidents Commission on Campus Unrest. (1970). *Report of the Presidents Commission on Campus Unrest.* Chicago: Commerce Clearing House.

Radzinowicz, Leon. (1968). *A History of English Criminal Law and its Administration from 1750* (v. 4). London: Stevens & Son.

Sashkin, M., and Kiser, K.J. (1991). *Total Quality Management.* Seabrook, MD.: Ducochon Press.

Scholtes, P.R. (1988). *The Team Handbook.* Madison, WI.: Joiner Associates.

Scott, M. S. (1986). *Managing for Success: A Police Chiefs Survival Guide.* Washington, DC: Police Executive Research Forum.

Selye, H. (1976). *The Stress of Life* (revised ed.). New York: McGraw-Hill.

Sheehan, R. and Cordner, G. W. (1995). *Police Administration* (3rd Ed.). Cincinnati, OH: Anderson.

Sherman, L.W., and Berk, R.A. (1984). *The Minneapolis Domestic Violence Experiment.* Washington, DC.: Police Foundation.

Simon, H. (1945). *Administrative Behavior.* New York: The Free Press.

Souryal, S. S. (1992). *Ethics in Criminal Justice: In Search of Truth.* Cincinnati, OH: Anderson.

Strecher, V.G. (1991). "Histories and Futures of Policing: Readings and Misreadings of Pivotal Present." *Police Forum,* Academy of Criminal justice Sciences Police Section, 1(1) (January).

Stojkovic, S., Kalinich, D. and Klofas, J. (1999). *The Administration and Management of Criminal Justice Organizations.* Third Edition. Prospect Heights, IL: Waveland Press.

Termer, A.R., and DeToro, I.J. (1992). *Total Quality Management.* Reading, MA.: Addison/Wesley.

Texas Department of Commerce. (1993). *Quality Texas: Investment for Survival.* Austin, Texas: State of Texas.

Trojanowicz, R. & Bucqueroux, B. (1990). *Community Policing: A Contemporary Perspective.* Cincinnati: Anderson Publishing Co.

Universal Training Systems Company. (1976). *How to Review and Evaluate Employee Performance: New Appraisal Techniques for Better Motivation.* Chicago: Dartnell.

Vaughn, J. R. (1989). *How to Rate Your Police Chief.* Washington, DC: Police Executive Research Forum.

Walker, S. (1989). *Sense and Nonsense About Crime* (2nd ed.). Pacific Grove, CA: Brooks/Cole Publishing Co.

Walton, M. (1986). *The Deming Management Method.* New York: Putnam Perigee.

Washington, George. (1796). "Farewell address to the People of the United States, September, 1796." In Delattre, E. J. 1996. *Character and Cops: Ethics in Policing,* Washington, DC: AEI Press, (page 34).

Williams, H. undated. Commentary on the video *Foot Patrol.* Crime File Video Series. Washington, DC: The Police Foundation and Television Station WETA.

Wycoff, M. A., and Skogan, W. K. (1993). *Community Policing in Madison: Quality From the Inside Out.* Washington, DC: National Institute of Justice.

RESOURCES

Community Policing Consortium; 1726 M Street, N.W., Suite 801, Washington, DC 20036; Telephone 800-833-3085, fax: 202-833-9295; URL address: www.communitypolicing.org

Crime Control Digest; Washington Crime News Services, 3702 Pender Drive, Suite 300, Fairfax, VA 22030-6066; Telephone: 800-422-9267 or 703-352-4811, fax: 703-352-2323

Federal Emergency Management Agency; 500 C Street SW, Washington, DC 20472; Telephone: (202) 646-4600; URL address: www.fema.gov

Government Technology; 9719 Lincoln Village Drive, Suite 500, Sacramento, CA 95827; Telephone: 916-363-5000, fax: 916-363-5197; URL address: www.govtech.net

Illinois Association of Chiefs of Police; 426 South Fifth Street, Suite 200, Springfield, IL 62701-1824; Telephone: 217-523-3765; URL address: www.ilchiefs.org

Illinois Association of County Officials; 302 East Illinois, New Berlin, IL 62670; Telephone: 217-488-6414

Illinois Criminal Justice Information Authority; 120 S. Riverside Plaza, Suite 1016 Chicago IL 60606; Telephone: 888-425-4248 or 312-793-8550, fax: 312-793-8422; URL address: www.icjia.org

Illinois Law Enforcement Executive Institute; Dr. Robert Fischer, Director, Western Illinois University; 1 University Circle; Macomb, IL 61455; Telephone: 309-298-2266, fax: 309-298-2215; URL address: www.cait.wiu.edu/iletsb

Illinois Law Enforcement Media Resource Center; Western Illinois University, 1 University Circle, Macomb, IL 61455; Telephone: 800-843-2690 or 309-298-2646, fax: 309-298-2642; URL address: www.ecnet.net/users/milemc

Illinois Municipal League; 500 East Capitol Avenue, Springfield, IL 62701; Telephone: 217-525-1220

Illinois Sheriff's Association; P. O. Box 263, Sherman, IL 62684; Telephone: 217-496-2371, fax: 217-496-2373

International Association of Chiefs of Police; 515 North Washington Street, Alexandria, VA 22314; Telephone: 703-836-6767 or 800-834-4227; URL address: www.theiacp.org

International Association of Women Police; North Deer Isle Road, Box 149, Deer Isle, ME 04627-9700; Telephone: 207-348-6976, fax: 207-348-6171; URL address: www.iawp.org

Jail and Prisoner Law Bulletin; Americans for Effective Law Enforcement, P. O. Box 75401, Chicago, IL 60656-1498; Telephone: 800-763-2802, fax: 800-763-3221; URL address: www.aele.org

National Criminal Justice Reference Service; Box 6000; Rockville, MD 20849; Telephone: 800-851-3420; URL address: www.ncjrs.org

National Institute of Justice; 810 Seventh Street, NW; Washington, DC 20531; Telephone: 202-307-2942; URL address: www.ojp.usdoj.gov/nij

National Law Enforcement and Corrections Technology Center; National Office: 2277 Research Boulevard, Rockville, MD 20850; Telephone: 800-248-2742, fax: 301-519-5149; URL address: www.nlectc.org

National Organization of Black Law Enforcement Executives (NOBLE); 4609 Pinecrest Office Park Drive, Suite F, Alexandria VA 22312-1442; Telephone: 703-658-1529, fax: 703-658-9479; URL address: www.noblenatl.org

National Sheriffs Association; 1450 Duke Street, Alexandria, VA 22314-3490; Telephone: 703-836-7827; URL address: www.sheriffs.org

Police Executive Research Forum (PERF); 1120 Connecticut Avenue NW, Suite 930, Washington, DC 20036; Telephone: 202-466-7820; URL address: www.policeforum.org

Police Labor Monthly; Justex Systems, Inc., P. O. Box 6224, Huntsville, TX 77342-6224; Telephone: 800-842-5203, fax: 936-294-0984; URL address: www.justex.com

Police Liability Reporter; Americans for Effective Law Enforcement, P. O. Box 75401, Chicago, IL 60656-1498; Telephone: 800-763-2802, fax: 800-763-3221; URL address: www.aele.org

A COURSE FOR NEW LAW ENFORCEMENT ADMINISTRATORS

MONDAY
7:00 - 8:00	Breakfast		
8:00 - 9:00	Welcome/Orientation	Dr. Robert Fischer	Director, ILEEI
		George Koertge	Exec Dir, IACP
9:00 -12:00	IL Law Enforcement	Dr. Thomas Jurkanin	Exec Dir, ILETSB
	Training and Standards	Chuck McDonald	Field Representative, ILETSB
	Board Staff	John Janssen	Asst Proj Dir, ILETSB
		Pat Vaughan	Deputy Dir, ILETSB
12:00 - 1:00	Lunch		
1:00 - 3:00	Principle-Based Leader Leadership	George Koertge	Exec Dir, IACP
3:00 - 3:15	Break		
3:15 - 5:00	Principle - Based Leadership (contd)	George Koertge	Exec Dir, IACP

TUESDAY
7:00 - 8:00	Breakfast		
8:00 -10:00	Progressive Discipline & Development	Don Slazinik	Dept of Public Safety OFallon
10:00 -12:00	Public Safety Issues	John Schlaf	Chief of Police Galesburg
12:00 - 1:00	Lunch		
1:00 - 3:00	<u>Concurrent Sessions</u>		
	Unions/Bargaining	Session A - Pat Vaughan	Dep Dir, ILETSB
	Alternatives for Small Community Policing	Session B - Robin Johnson	Dir, Ill Center for Competitive Govt
3:00 - 3:15	Break		
3:15 - 5:00	Mission/Infrastructure	Mark Field	Chief of Police Wheaton

WEDNESDAY

7:00 - 8:00	Breakfast		
8:00 -10:00	Legal Issues	Russell Laine	Chief of Police Algonquin
10:00 - 1:00	Policing Trends for the Immediate Future	Dr. Clyde Crohkhite	Professor, Law Enforcement and Justice Administration, Western Illinois University

Working Lunch

1:00 - 3:00	Illinois Legislative Update	Paul Dollins	Legislative Liaison, IACP
		Don Hays	IL Appellate Prosecutors Office
3:00 - 3:15	Break		
3:15 - 5:00	Support Agency Panel	Federal Bureau of Investigation Illinois State Police Secretary of State Department of Corrections	

THURSDAY

7:00 - 8:00	Breakfast		
8:00 -11:00	Budget Planning	George Dulzo	Chief of Police Hickory Hills
11:00 -12:00	Legal Issues and Liability	Don Soufal	General Counsel Chicago Police Dept
12:00 - 1:00	Lunch		
1:00 - 3:00	Legal Issues and Liability (continued)	Don Zoufal	General Counsel
3:00 - 3:15	Break		
3:15 - 5:00	ILETSB: Special Projects/ Training/Grants	Dr. Robert J. Fischer	Director, ILEEI

FRIDAY

7:00 - 8:00	Breakfast		
8:00 -10:00	The Community	Raymond Rose	Chief of Police Mundelein
10:00 -12:00	Politics	John Millner	Chief of Police Elmhurst
12:00 - 1:00	Lunch		
1:00 - 3:00	Communication	John Miller	Chief of Police Elmhurst
3:00 - 4:00	Graduation		

NAME INDEX

Albrecht, K., 119, 120, 125
Bittner, E., 47
Bolman, L. G., 6
Bopp, W., 64
Cordner, G. W., 61, 108, 111, 113, 115, 117
Deal, T. E., 6
Delattre, E. J., 15
Eck, J. E., 111
Fayol, H., 7
Goldstein, H., 15, 16
Gore, A., 118
Greenwood, P., 111
Hanna, D., 31
Hoover, L. T., 109
Jones, T. L., 64
Kelling, G. L., 111
Kiser, K. J., 119
Likert, R., 52
Lindbloom, C. E., 8
Mahtesian, C., quoted xviii
McCarthy, W., 16
Meade, M., quoted xv
Mintzberg, H., 3, 4, 52

Moore, M. H., 60, 61
Morgan, B., 36
Oncken, W., 35
Ouchi, W. G., 121
Peters, T. J., 44
Petersilia, J., 111
Pollack, J. M., 15
Radzinowicz, L., 107
Sashkin, M., 119
Selye, H., 26
Sheehan, R., 61
Simon, H., 7, 8, 52
Skogan, W. K., 116
Stephens, D. W., 60, 61
Trojanowicz, R., 108
Washington, G., 29
Waterman, R. H., 44
Weber, M., 6
Whisenand, P., 64
Wilson, O. W., 128
Wycoff, M. A., 116
Zemke, R., 119, 120, 125

SUBJECT INDEX

A

Accessibility of police administrator
(*see also* Time management)
    call screening, 33
    open-door-policy by appointment, 38
    scheduling, 33
    time management vs. accessibility, 42
    walk-in visits, 33
Accounting techniques and policing, 123–27
(*see also* TQM)
Administrative decisionmaking, 6–9 (*see also* Management)
    information acquisition, 6
    overview of evolution, 6–9
    rational management, 7
Alcohol abuse, 27–28
Appendix
    course for new law enforcement administrators, 155–56
    resource listings, 153–54

B

Bounded rationality, 8
Budget management, 85–96
    budget analysis steps, 86
        goal identification, 86
        relating goals to specific programs, 86
        relating goals to resource requirements, 87
    relating resource inputs to budget dollars, 87
    budget officer, 85–86
    budget process, 91–96, 136–46
        city manager team, 92–93, 136–46
        community-wide priorities, 92–93, 136–46
        suggestions for budgetary cooperation, 92–93
    justification, 93–94
    projection of 3–5 years, 91
    clothing allowances, 91
    labor contracts, 91
    overtime, 91
    personnel expenses, 87, 91
    sheriff's budget considerations, 91–92
        civil processes, 92
        court security, 92
        inmate transportation, 92
        jail operations, 92,
        officer's of the court, 92
    sources of revenue, 94–96
        community gifts for special needs, 95
        economic development, 94
        grants, 95
        sales tax and user revenue, 94
    operational planning, budgeting re programs, 86–88
    objectives and goals, 86–88
    personnel expenses, 87, 91
    program alternatives analysis, 88–91
        allocation of activities to cost columns, 89, 90
        programs' effectiveness assessment, 88–91
        allocation of resources, 89
        effectiveness vs. workload demands, 88–89
        organizational units and output categories, 90
        costing-out and effectiveness, 90
    strategic planning, 85–88
    utilization of police human resources, 87–88
Bureaucracy
    elements of effective, 6–7
    routine, standardized procedures, 49, 52

C

Ceremonial roles, 5
Chamber of Commerce and business groups, 134

Citizen Police Academy, 23
City manager, 92–93, 141
Civil liability of police executives, 64–79
   civil lawsuit requirements, 70
   employee suits, 74–79
      ways to minimize personal civil liability, 76
   individual rights and social need for order, 66
   lawsuit vs. liability, 70–71
   legal defenses, 72–74
      cause of action, 73
      constitutional rights, 74
      factual basis, 73
      qualified immunity, 73–74
      respondeat superior, 74
   litigation overview, 64–67
   public accountability vs. legal liability, 65
   public official liability insurance, 72
   sovereign immunity abrogation, 66–67
   suits as impetus to examine policy, 70
   tort suits, 67–70 (*see also* Tort suits)
   visibility and image, 64–65
Code of Ethics, 17, 55–56
Collective bargaining, 103–6
   maintenance of standards clause, 104
   management rights, 103–5
   managers as full participants, 103–6
Communication skills, 36–37
   (*see also* Leadership development)
   crossing divisional lines, 37
   formal and informal structures, 37–38
   open-door policy, 38
   vertical and horizontal flow, 37
Community-based policing, 14–15, 48–53, 107–17
   acceptable vs. unacceptable ie gratuities, 14–15, 55–56
   defining myriad of focus points, 43–45, 107–16
   efficiency, 52–53
   four dimensions model, 108–16 (*see also* Community policing four dimensions model)
   implementation, 116–17
   information processing, 52
   intervention techniques
      arrest, 49
      authoritative persuasion, 49
      extended counseling, 49
      social counseling, 49
      social referral, 49
      structural/environmental changes, 49
   long-term beat complacency, 15
   maintaining peacefulness, 47
   order maintenance, 45–48
      (*see also* Order maintenance)
   problem-oriented vs. community-oriented techniques, 48
   public perception of police as crime control, 50
   sustained vs. temporal order, 48–53
   Ten Principles of Community Policing, 108
Community policing four dimensions model, 108–16
   organizational approach, 115–16
      decentralization, 115
      Geographic Information Systems, 116
      hierarchy flattening, 116
      information, 115, 116
      structure, 115, 116
   philosophical approach, 108–11
      broad police function, 109
         quality of life activities, 109
      citizen input, 108
      neighborhood beat police, 109–11
      neighborhood needs assessment, 109
      personal service, 109
      social service, 109
      targeted enforcement, 109
   strategic approach, 111–13
      beat officers and follow-up investigations, 112
      crime prevention, 113
      differential response, 112, 123
      geographic focus, 111
         long-term problems response, 112
         specialist teams, 112
      investigative teams focused on offenders, 112
      prevention emphasis, 111
      proactive orientation, 113
         directed patrol, 113

        patterns and problems, 113
        reoriented operations, 111
    tactical approach, 113–15
        beat manager characteristics, 115, 116
        partnerships, 113, 114
        positive interaction, 113–14
        problem solving, 113, 114–15
        SARA model, 115
Community influence
    focus groups' advocacy, 38
    networking with public service peers, 38
    priority input via community groups, 38
    total quality management and
        policing, 118–27
Competing constituencies, xviii, 32–33, 38
Corruption (*see also* Ethical behavior)
    definition, 15
    external and internal influences, 16
    influences, 14–16
        improper political interference, 16
        intangible, 16
        monetary, 14–15
        organized criminal interests, 16
        police assignments, 16
        police discretion, 16
        police work nature, 16
        unenforceable laws, 16
    intangible influences, 16
    rooting out and acknowledgement of, 16
Corruption, determination
    investigation of corrupters, 16
    quid pro quo, 16
    totality-of-circumstances rule, 16
Counting techniques and policing, 123–27
Court security, 82
Criminal justice agencies,
    relationship, 143–44
Crisis planning, 83–84
    coordination of emergency services, 83
    emergency management teams, 83–84
    natural or man-made events, 83
    response plan, 83–84
    sensational event characteristics, 84
    test, evaluate, update, 83
Customer satisfaction and policing, 122–23
    (*see also* TQM)
Customer service and policing, 119–27

(*see also* TQM)

D

Death messages and procedures, 43, 52
Decisionmaking, 6–9
    information acquisition, 6
Delegation, 5, 34–35
    management trends, 34
    of authority, 20–21, 35
    of responsibility, 34–35
    work-related delegation initiatives, 35
Differential response, 112, 123, 125
Disciplinary actions, 77–79
    administrative due process, 78
    behavior and disciplinary
        procedures model, 77
    determination of actions for
        investigation, 77
    errors vs. rule violations, 36, 77
    internal affairs unit, 77–78
    investigating official, 77
    procedural due process, 78
Disseminator managerial role, 4
(*see also* Managerial roles)
Disturbance handler, 4
(*see also* Managerial roles)
Drugs, prescription abuse, 27–28

E

Education and training, 12, 21–24
    knowledge of
        agency-community history, 21
        assessment of program needs, 23
        financial aspects of municipality, 21
        formal training programs, 23–24
        informal training programs, 23–24
        Internet accessibility, 23
        professional journals accessibility, 23
        roll-call training/teaching, 23
    police organization memberships, 22
    professional journals, 22
    program effectiveness evaluation, 23
    technology, 21–23
    training and education, 22–24
        formal training programs, 23–24

informal training programs, 23-24
unions and labor relations, 22
Efficiency, 52-53
Eighth Amendment suits
　prisoner suits of cruel and unusual
　　punishment, 69
Elected officials, relationship with, 136-41
　(*see also* Political systems)
　budget support, 138
　checks and balances and law
　　enforcement, 138-39
　city council/board, 136
　city manager/mayoral relations,
　　138, 141-42
　communication skills, 136, 140
　political statesmanship, 137
　reporting requirements, 138
Employee associations, 97-106
　adversarial relationship, 98-106
　collective bargaining, 103-6
　　maintenance of standards clause, 104
　　management rights, 103-5
　　managers as full participants, 103-6
　development, 98-103
　duality of officer/union rep, 97-98
　grievance system, 99
　management by walking around, 102-3
　meeting settings, 99
　morale, 100-1
Entrepreneur managerial role, 4
　(*see also* Managerial roles)
Escapees, response plans, 82
Ethical behavior, 11-30
　(*see also* Ten commandments)
　Code of Ethics, 17, 55-56
　corruption, seeds of, 15
　　(*see also* Corruption)
　　acceptable vs. unacceptable ie
　　　gratuities, 14-15, 55-56
　　community-based policing, 15
　　external vs. internal influences, 16
　　organizational influences, 15
　integrity, 15-30, 56
　　self-questions (3), 15
　mission/value statements, 17, 42-56
　recruitment and retention programs,
　　15, 55

training with emphasis on ethics, 15
Executive training programs
　FBI Academy, xix
　LEEDS, xix
　Northwestern Traffic Institute, xix
　Southern Police Institute, xix

F

Federal Bureau of Investigation
　Academy, xix
Federal and state labor, personnel
　statutes, 68, 70, 75-79
　employment discrimination suits, 67, 75
　fair employment, 70
　sexual harassment, 70
　state jurisdiction re public
　　employees' rights, 75
Figurehead managerial role, 4
　(*see also* Managerial roles)
Fire department, relationship
　with police, 143
First Amendment suits
　adverse personnel actions, 69
　free speech violations, 69
Fourteenth Amendment
　deprivation of due process, 69
Fourth Amendment suits
　false arrest, 68
　illegal search, 68
　use of force, 68
Functional approach, 7

G

Gratuities, acceptable vs. unacceptable,
　14-15, 55-56
Grounds and buildings maintenance and
　support, 81-82

H

Healthy lifestyle, 12, 24-28
　annual medical exams, 24, 25
　death, leading causes of, 24-25
　exercise program, 24, 26, 41-42
　limitation on use of tobacco, alcohol,

etc., 24, 27–28
  personal embarrassment wounds, 28
  maintaining outside life, 24, 28
  nutritional balances, 24, 25
  stress management, 24, 26–27
    (see also Stress management)
  weight restrictions, 24–26
Human resources, 57–64
  personnel training and career
    development, 59–61
    in-service training, 59–60
      career development program, 60
      changes in laws, procedures,
        policies, 59–60
      correction officers re entry level
        positions, 60–61
      merit pay incentives, 60
    performance evaluations, 61–64
    promotion screening and boards, 61
    specialist positions, 61
    training needs assessment pointers, 60
      communication skills, 60
      managing mentally disturbed
        individuals, 60
      pursuit driving, 60
      report writing, 60
  recruiting and hiring, 57–59
    community's diversity, reflection, 58
    front-line actions of officers, 58
    mechanical skills, 59
    people skills, 59
    selection processes, 59
    training, 59
      departmental field training, 59
      State mandated courses, 59

I

Illinois Association of Chiefs of Police, 22
Illinois Association of County Officials, 22
Illinois Law Enforcement Executive
  Institute, xxii, 22
Illinois Law Enforcement Training and
  Standards Board, xix, 82
Illinois Municipal League, 22
Illinois Sheriffs Association, 22, 82
Inductive vs. deductive approach to
  management, 3
Influences for corruption, 14–16
  improper political interference, 16
  intangible, 16
  monetary, 14–15
  organized criminal interests, 16
  police assignments, 16
  police discretion, 16
  police work nature, 16
  unenforceable laws, 16
Information access, status and authority, 6
Information dissemination, 5–6
Information via oral sources, 5
Integrity, 15–31, 56
  (see also Ten commandments)
  Code of Ethics, 17, 55–56
  ethical behavior, 11–30, 55–56
  lead by example, 31
  mission/value statements, 17
  self-questions (3), 15
Internal affairs unit, 77–78
  administrative due process, 78
  tour of duty, 78
International Association of
  Chiefs of Police, 55
Internet, 23
Intervention techniques and temporal
  order maintenance, 47
In-service training, 59–60
  career development program, 60
    merit pay incentives, 60
  changes in laws, procedures,
    policies, 59–60
  correction officers re entry level
    positions, 60–61
  promotion screening and boards, 61
  specialist positions, 61
  training needs assessment pointers, 60
    communication skills, 60
    managing mentally disturbed
      individuals, 60
    pursuit driving, 60
    report writing, 60

J

Jails, security plan, 82

Job security and performance
   incentives, 16, 121-22, 136

L

Law enforcement and order maintenance,
   45-48
Law Enforcement Executive Development
   School (LEEDS), xix
Law Enforcement Training Standards Board,
   xv, xvi
Leadership development, 31-42
   communication skills, 36-37
   competing constituencies, 32-33
   delegating, 20-21, 34-35
      (see also Delegation)
   informal organization structure, 37-38
      (see also Organizational structure)
   mentoring, 21, 34 policy manuals, 35-36
   skills identification, 31-32
   time management, 33
      (see also Time management)
Leadership skills
   administration vs. street operations, 31
   attributes, 31
      technical knowledge, 31
   community appearances, 31
   core values and expectations, 31
   hands-on management style, 31
   lead by example, 31
   media relations, 31
   visionary, 31
   vs. management, 31
   walking around style, 31
Legislative branch
   checks and balances on law enforcement,
      138-39
   legislation, influencing, 145-46
Litigation
   civil lawsuit requirements, 70
   civil liability of police executives, 64-79
   employee suits, 74-79
      ways to minimize personal civil
         liability, 76
   individual rights and social need
      for order, 66
   lawsuit vs. liability, 70-71
   legal defenses, 72-74
      cause of action, 73
      constitutional rights, 74
      factual basis, 73
      qualified immunity, 73-74
      respondeat superior, 74
   overview, 64-67
   public accountability vs. legal liability, 65
   public official liability insurance, 72
   sovereign immunity abrogation, 66-67
   suits as impetus to examine policy, 70
   tort suits, 67-70 (see also Tort suits)
   visibility and image, 64-65
Local government
   elected officials, 136-41
      budget support, 138
      checks and balances and law
         enforcement, 138-39
      city council/board, 136
      city manager/mayoral relations,
         138, 141-42
      communication skills, 136, 140
      political statesmanship, 137
      reporting requirements, 138
   expectations and demands on
      department, xviii
   influence on chief executive tenure,
      xviii, 33
Logical incrementalism, 8-9

M

Management
   administrative decisionmaking, 6-9
      (see also Administrative decisionmaking)
   ceremonial roles, 5
   computer data vs. judgment, intuition, 5
   information access, status and authority, 6
   information dissemination, 5-6
   information via oral sources, 5
   leadership skill development, 31-42
   logical incrementalism, 8-9
   management rights re collective
      bargaining, 105
   managerial roles, 3-6
   organizational science, evolution, 6-10
   policy input by employees, 34

priority hierarchy, 4–5
symbolically sensitive issues, 5
ten commandments of personal/
  professional conduct, 11–30
  (*see also* Ten commandments)
time demands, 4, 5
total quality management: culture,
  customers, counting, 119–27
    limitations to policing, 119–27
Managerial myths
  delegation of duties, 5
  information age accessibility, 5
  information via documentation, 5
  limited access to constituency, 5
  time management, 4, 5
Managerial roles, 4–6
  (*see also* Police chief)
  decisional, 4
  informational, 4
  interpersonal, 4
  logical incrementalism advocacy, 9
  inductive vs. deductive, 3–5
Management trends
  management by objectives, 9
  organizational development, 9
  participatory management, 34
  planning-programming-budgeting
    systems, 9
  quality circles, 34
  reinventing corporation/government, 9
  team building, 34
  team management, 34
  total quality management,
    9–10, 118–27
  zero-based budgeting, 9
Mentoring, 21, 34
  re favoritism, 33
Morale, 100–1

N

National Institute of Justice
  on-line publications, 23
National Labor Relations Act, 75
  application to public employees, 75
National Sheriff's Association, 82
Neighborhood beat police, 109–10
  allocation of resources, 111
  complacency, 15
  incentives to empower citizens, 110
  ownership, 110
  permanent assignment, 110
Negotiator, 4, 31 (*see also* Managerial roles)
News media, 129–30
  guidelines, 130
Northwestern Traffic Institute Staff and
  Command and Police Supervisors
  School, xix

O

Objective rationality, 7
Order maintenance vs. law
  enforcement, 45–48
  boundary crossovers, 46–47
  scene objective and intervention
    technique, 46–47
  temporal hierarchy, 45–48
    conflict management, 45–48
    law enforcement, 45–48
    public service/safety, 45–48
Organized anarchy, 5, 8
Organizational science, 4–6
  decisionmaking, 6–9
    bounded rationality, 8
    objective rationality, 7
    subjective rationality, 7
  functional approach, 7
  logical incrementalism, 8–9
  myths, 4–6
  organized anarchy, 5, 8
  political processes, 6, 8, 33
  principles approach, 6
  satisficing, 8, 9
    antidotes, 9–10
  systems approach, 6
  total quality management: culture,
    customers, counting, 119–27
    limitations to policing, 119–27
  Weber's ideal bureaucracy, 6–7
Organizational structure, 37–38
  chain-of-command, 37
  formal structure, 37
  informal structure, 37

leadership by personality, 37
span of control, 37
unity of command, 37

P

Peacekeeping, 46–48
Performance evaluations, 61–64
    appeal process, 63–64
    development goals, 62
    evaluation guidelines, 63
    evaluation tools, 61
    evaluator comfort level, 63
    informal review, 63
    job description components, 62
    merit pay vs. longevity, 61
    objectives, 61
    overall job performance, 62
    periodic assessments of system, 64
    performance logs, 62
    task evaluation, 61
    tasks, skills, knowledge of job, 64
Physical fitness
    exercise program, 24, 26, 41–42
Planning programming budgeting systems (PPBS), 86 (*see also* Budget management)
Police administrators/executives
    applied application and practice, xvi
    balance between expedience and planning, 3
    ceremonial duties, 5
    logical incrementalism advocacy, 9–10
    managerial roles, 3–6
        (*see also* Managerial roles)
    police mission: development, adherence, 43–56 (*see also* Police mission)
    procurement process and ethical dilemmas, 17
        (*see also* Procurement process)
    ten commandments of personal/professional conduct, 11–30
        (*see also* Ten commandments)
        ethical standards definition, 11–12
        overview, 11–12
    tenure, xvi, 33
    total quality management: culture, customers, counting, 119–27
    limitations to policing, 119–27
Police chief (*see also* Management; Police administrators; Political systems)
    ceremonial duties, 5
    chamber and business groups, 134
    city government departments, 142–44
    city manager, 141–42
    community relations, 128–33
        correspondence, 130–31
        surveys, 131–33
    corruption, influences of, 16
    elected officials, 136–41
        budget support, 138
        checks and balances and law enforcement, 138–39
        city council/board, 136
        city manager/mayoral relations, 138, 141–42
        communication skills, 136, 140
        legislation, influencing, 145–46
        political statesmanship, 137
        reporting requirements, 138
    influence of processes on police administrator, 6, 8, 17, 33, 128–46
    managerial roles, 4, 11–30, 128–46
        (*see also* Managerial roles)
    neighborhood associations, 133–34
    news media, 129–30
        guidelines, 130
    partisan politics influence, 128
    police chief job security, xviii, 16, 121–22, 136
    public promotion of crime reduction progress, 129
    rate of turnover factors, xviii
    service clubs, 135
    special interest groups, 135
    ten commandments of personal/professional conduct, 11–30
        (*see also* Ten commandments)
    total quality management limitations, 118–26
Police mission statement, 43–56
    Code of Ethics, 17, 55–56
    community-oriented policing, 48–53
    (*see also* Community policing)
    evaluation reference, 54

information processing, 52
institutionalizing values, 55
organizational values, 53–55
shared vision, 53
stakeholder development, 53
problem-oriented vs. community-oriented techniques, 48
public perception of police as crime control, 50
sustained order vs. temporal order, 48
intervention techniques
   arrest, 49
   authoritative persuasion, 49
   extended counseling, 49
   social counseling, 49
   social referral, 49
structural/environmental changes, 49
defining myriad of focus points, 43–45
maintaining peacefulness, 47
order maintenance, 45–48
   (see also Order maintenance)
overview, 43–45
Police Research Forum, xviii
Policy manuals, 35–6
   evolving not static, 35
   policies, definition, 35
   procedures, definition, 35
   rules and regulations, definition, 35
      violations and disciplinary actions, 36
      (see also Disciplinary actions)
   legal reviews, 36
   scheduled reviews for conformance, 36
Political statesmanship, 137
Political systems
   chamber and business groups, 134
   city government departments, 142–44
   city manager, 141–42
   community relations, 128–33
      correspondence, 130–31
      surveys, 131–33
   corruption, influences of, 16
   elected officials, 136–41
      budget support, 138
      checks and balances and law enforcement, 138–39
      city council/board, 136
      city manager/mayoral relations, 138, 141–42

      communication skills, 136, 140
      political statesmanship, 137
      reporting requirements, 138
   influence of processes on police administrator, 6, 8, 17, 33, 128–46
   neighborhood associations, 133–34
   news media, 129–30
      guidelines, 130
   partisan politics influence, 128
   police chief job security, xviii, 16, 121–22, 136
   public promotion of crime reduction progress, 129
   influence/interference into police administrator's role, 17, 33
   service clubs, 135
   special interest groups, 135
POSDCORB, 7
Principles approach
   organizational coordination, 7
   POSDCORB, 7
Procurement processes and litigation, 17
   emergency procurements, 17
   noncompetitive grants, 17
   procurement divisions, 17
   request requirements ie vague, 17
   short time period for proposal submission, 17
   sole sourcing, 17
   use of unofficially preferred vendors, 17
Public vs. private sector employees
   collective bargaining rights, 75
   Equal Employment Opportunity Act, 75
   Fair Labor Standards Act, 75
   OSHA application, 75
   National Labor Relations Act, 75

Q

Quality management (see TQM)

R

Rational management, 7
Resource allocator, 4
(see also Managerial roles)
Routine, standardized bureaucratic responses, 49, 52

S

Sanitation department, relationship, 143
SARA model, 115
    scanning, analyze, response, assessment, 115
Satisficing, 8, 9
    antidotes, 9–10
Schools, relationship with police, 142–43
    D.A.R.E. programs, 143
    liaison efforts, 143
    school resource officers, 143
Service clubs, 135
Sheriff (*see also* Management;
  Police administrators)
    budget considerations, 91–92
      (*see also* Budget management)
      civil processes, 92
      court security, 92
      inmate transportation, 92
      jail operations, 92,
      officer's of the court, 92
    ceremonial duties, 5
    chamber and business groups, 134
    city government departments, 142–44
    city manager, 141–42
    community relations, 128–33
      correspondence, 130–31
      surveys, 131–33
    corruption, influences of, 16
    elected officials, 136–41
      budget support, 138
      checks and balances and law
        enforcement, 138–39
      city council/board, 136
      city manager/mayoral relations,
        138, 141–42
      communication skills, 136, 140
      influencing legislation, 145–46
      political statesmanship, 137
      reporting requirements, 138
    election as sheriff, 139
    influence of processes on police
      administrator, 6, 8, 17, 33, 128–46
    managerial roles, 4, 11–30, 128–46
      (*see also* Managerial roles)
    neighborhood associations, 133–34
    news media, 129–30
      guidelines, 130
    partisan politics influence, 128
    police chief job security, xviii, 16,
      121–22, 136
    political role, 139, 144–45
    public promotion of crime reduction
      progress, 129
    rate of turnover factors, xviii
    service clubs, 135
    special interest groups, 135
    ten commandments of
      personal/professional conduct, 11–30
      (*see also* Ten commandments)
    total quality management
      limitations, 118–26
Simon's categories of decisionmaking
    bounded rationality, 8
    objective rationality, 7
    subjective rationality, 7
Southern Police Institute, xix
Sovereign immunity doctrine, 66–67
    (*see also* Civil liability)
Special interest groups, 135
Specialized units
    community relations, 41
    investigations, 41
    juvenile, 41
    metropolitan enforcement groups, 41
    narcotics, 41
    rotations, 41
    tactical operations, 41
    traffic, 41
Spirituality, 21
Spokesperson managerial role, 4
    (*see also* Managerial roles)
Staffing allocation, 40–41
Statistics and policing, 123–27
    total quality management
      limitations, 123–27
Stress management, 24, 26–27
    hobbies, 27
    physiological reactions, 26–27
    relaxation exercises, meditation, 27
    workshops, 27
Subjective rationality, 7
Supervisory training, 39–42

liability training, 39
meetings, 40
roll call training, 39–40
   information dissemination mistakes, 39–40
specialized units, 41
   rotation mechanism, 41
staff and command school, 39
staffing allocation, 40–41
team building, 34, 40
Surveys, community
   sample questions, 132–33
   structuring, 131–33
Symbolically sensitive issues, 5

T

Team building, 34, 40
   core identifiers, 40
Technology, 79–80
   citizen expectations, 79
   evaluation and assessment process for new, 79–80
   information systems, 80–81
      artificial intelligence 80, 81
      computer aided dispatch, 80
      crime analysis, 80, 81
      geographic information systems, 80, 81
      information management, 80–81
      jail management, 80
   maintenance and testing procedures, 80
   911 systems, 79
   911 systems, enhanced, 79
Temporal order maintenance hierarchy, 45–48
   conflict management, 45–48
   law enforcement, 45–48
   public service/safety, 45–48
Ten commandments of personal/professional conduct, 11–30, 55–56
   accept assistance, 12, 20–21
      command staff, 20
      confidante, 21
      delegation of authority, 20–21
      participatory management, 20
      spirituality, 21
   day's pay for day-and-a-half work, 12–14, 56
      long, unmeasurable, team-building hours, 13–14
   healthy lifestyle, 12, 24–28
      annual medical exams, 24, 25
      death, leading causes of, 24–25
      exercise program, 24, 26
      limitation on use of tobacco, alcohol, etc., 24, 27–28
      personal embarrassment wounds, 28
      maintaining outside life, 24, 28
      nutritional balances, 24, 25
      stress management, 24, 26–27
      (*see also* Stress management)
      weight restrictions, 24–26
   integrity, maintain and promote, 12, 14–17, 29, 55–56
      corruption seeds, 14–17
      (*see also* Corruption)
      community-based policing, 15
      organizational influences, 15
   ethical behavior guidelines, 16–17, 29, 5–56 (*see also* Ethical behavior)
   gift-in-kind, gratuities and promotional beneficiaries, 14–15, 55–56
   knowledge, 12, 21–24
   (*see also* Education and training)
      agency-community history, 21
      assessment of program needs, 23
      financial aspects of municipality, 21
      formal training programs, 23–24
      informal training programs, 23–24
      Internet accessibility, 23
      professional journals accessibility, 23
      roll-call training/teaching, 23
      police organization memberships, 22
      professional journals, 22
      program effectiveness evaluation, 23
      technology, 21–23
      training and education, 22–24
         formal training programs, 23–24
         informal training programs, 23–24
      unions and labor relations, 22
   personal goals, 12, 29
      assessment of personal and professional, 29
   positive image, 12, 18

cheerleader to the troops, 18
countermand negative external forces 18
morale, 18
recognition of others' contributions, 18
set the tone, 18, 29
practice what you preach, 12, 28
talk the talk, walk the walk, 12
remain committed, 12, 18–19
goals, mission, values, 18
risk-taking pitfalls, 18–19
respect and be respected, 12, 19–20
service vs. success, 20
Time management
call screening, 33
scheduling, 33
walk-in visits, 33
Tobacco products' abuse, 27–28
Top down leadership, 11–30, 55
Tort suits, 67–70 (*see also* Civil liability)
common law torts, 68
jail injuries, 68
pursuit driving collisions, 68
constitutional torts, 68
burden of proof, 69
deliberately indifferent, 69
Eighth Amendment violations, 68
First Amendment violations, 69
Fourteenth Amendment violations, 69
Fourth Amendment violations, 68
individual/agency liability
distinction, 69–70
1983 suits, 68–70
Federal and state labor, personnel
statutes, 68, 70
employment discrimination suits, 67
fair employment, 70
sexual harassment, 70
Monell v. New York City Dept. of Social Services, 67
scope of employment immunity,
indemnity, 68
sovereign immunity doctrine, 66–67
state statute regulation, 67
tort definition, 68
TQM (total quality management),
9–10, 118–27
accounting applications, 123–27
application limitations to policing, 119–27
cautions, 118–19
characteristics of service, 120
core elements, 119
culture, customers, counting, 119–27
limitations to policing, 119–27
customer service, 119–27
life-time job security element, 121
statistical measures, 123–27
Traffic citations and procedure, 52
Turnover, rate of, xviii
factors
competing constituencies, xviii, 32–33
demands and expectations of
departments, xviii
perception as part of problem vs.
solution, xviii

U

United States Marshal Service, 82

W

Weber's ideal bureaucracy, 6–7
fully informed, 6–7
rational management, 7
Work ethic, 12–14, 56
(*see also* Ten commandments)
Wrongful behavior
acknowledgement of individuals, 19
commitment to agency, 20

Z

Zero-based budgeting, 86

Charles C Thomas
PUBLISHER • LTD.

P.O. Box 19265
Springfield, IL 62794-9265

Book Savings (on separate titles only)
Save 10%!
Save 15%!
Save 20%!

- Colaprete, Frank A.—**INTERNAL INVESTIGATIONS: A Practitioner's Approach.** '07, 332 pp. (7x10), 61 il.

- Schlesinger, Louis B.—**EXPLORATIONS IN CRIMINAL PSYCHOPATHOLOGY: Clinical Syndromes With Forensic Implications.** (2nd Ed.) '07, 432 pp. (7 x 10), 3 il., 10 tables.

- Flowers, R. Barri—**SEX CRIMES: Perpetrators, Predators, Prostitutes, and Victims.** (2nd Ed.) '06, 314 pp. (7 x 10), 19 il., 18 tables.

- Mendell, Ronald L.—**HOW TO DO FINANCIAL ASSET INVESTIGATIONS: A Practical Guide for Private Investigators, Collections Personnel, and Asset Recovery Specialists.** (3rd Ed.) '06, 226 pp. (7 x 10), 13 il., 13 tables.

- Roberts, Albert R. & David W. Springer—**SOCIAL WORK IN JUVENILE AND CRIMINAL JUSTICE SETTINGS.** (3rd Ed.) '06, 462 pp. (8 x 10), 7 il., (1 in color), 17 tables, paper.

- Barker, Tom—**POLICE ETHICS: Crisis in Law Enforcement.** (2nd Ed.) '06, 126 pp. (7 x 10), 1 table, $39.95, hard, $24.95, paper.

- Decker, Kathleen P.—**FIT, UNFIT OR MISFIT? How To Perform Fitness for Duty Evaluations in Law Enforcement Professionals.** '06, 284 pp. (7 x 10), 3 il., 43 tables, $61.95, hard, $41.95, paper.

- Hendricks, James E. & Bryan D. Byers—**CRISIS INTERVENTION IN CRIMINAL JUSTICE/SOCIAL SERVICE.** (4th Ed.) '06, 410 pp. (7 x 10), 4 tables, $77.95, hard, $55.95, paper.

- Jurkanin, Thomas J. and Terry G. Hillard—**CHICAGO POLICE: An Inside View—The Story of Superintendent Terry G. Hillard.** '06, 252 pp. (7 x 10), $61.95, hard, $39.95, paper.

- Kolman, John A.—**PATROL RESPONSE TO CONTEMPORARY PROBLEMS: Enhancing Performance of First Responders Through Knowledge and Experience.** '06, 272 pp. (8 x 10), 86 il., $59.95, hard, $34.95, paper.

- MacHovec, Frank—**PRIVATE INVESTIGATION AND SECURITY SCIENCE: A Scientific Approach.** (3rd Ed.) '06, 204 pp. (7 x 10), $52.95, hard, $32.95, paper.

- Paton, Douglas & David Johnston—**DISASTER RESILIENCE: An Integrated Approach.** '06, 344 pp. (7 x 10), 22 il., 9 tables, $68.95, hard, $48.95, paper.

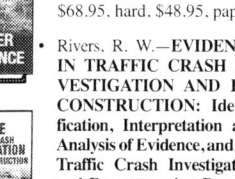

- Rivers, R. W.—**EVIDENCE IN TRAFFIC CRASH INVESTIGATION AND RECONSTRUCTION: Identification, Interpretation and Analysis of Evidence, and the Traffic Crash Investigation and Reconstruction Process.** '06, 324 pp. (8 x 10), 175 il., 13 tables, $86.95, hard, $56.95, paper.

- Rowe, Tina Lewis—**A PREPARATION GUIDE FOR THE ASSESSMENT CENTER METHOD.** '06, 268 pp. (7 x 10), $39.95, spiral (paper).

- Sanders, William P.—**LAW ENFORCEMENT FUNERAL MANUAL: A Practical Guide for Law Enforcement Agencies When Faced with the Death of a Member of Their Department.** (2nd Ed.) '06, 136 pp. (7 x 10), 2 il., $25.95, spiral (paper).

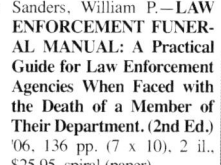

- Williams, Howard E.—**INVESTIGATING WHITE-COLLAR CRIME: Embezzlement and Financial Fraud.** (2nd Ed.) '06, 362 pp. (7 x 10), 31 tables, $69.95, hard, $49.95, paper.

- Woody, Robert Henley—**SEARCH AND SEIZURE: The Fourth Amendment for Law Enforcement Officers.** '06, 182 pp. (7 x 10), $43.95, hard, $28.95, paper.

- Bender, Lewis G., Thomas J. Jurkanin, Vladimir A. Sergevnin, & Jerry L. Dowling—**CRITICAL ISSUES IN POLICE DISCIPLINE: Case Studies.** '05, 156 pp. (7 x 10), $38.95, hard, $23.95, paper.

- McDevitt, Daniel S.—**MANAGING THE INVESTIGATIVE UNIT.** '05, 210 pp. (7 x 10), 2 tables, $51.95, hard, $31.95, paper.

- Moriarty, Laura J.—**CRIMINAL JUSTICE TECHNOLOGY IN THE 21st CENTURY.** (2nd Ed.) '05, 334 pp. (7 x 10), 5 il., 15 tables, $64.95, hard, $44.95, paper.

- Nicholson, William C.—**HOMELAND SECURITY LAW AND POLICY.** '05, 410 pp. (8 x 10), 9 il., 7 tables, $91.95, hard, $61.95, paper.

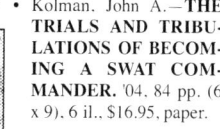

- Kolman, John A.—**THE TRIALS AND TRIBULATIONS OF BECOMING A SWAT COMMANDER.** '04, 84 pp. (6 x 9), 6 il., $16.95, paper.

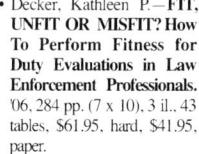

5 easy ways to order!

PHONE: 1-800-258-8980 or (217) 789-8980
FAX: (217) 789-9130
EMAIL: books@ccthomas.com
Web: www.ccthomas.com
MAIL: Charles C Thomas • Publisher, Ltd. P.O. Box 19265 Springfield, IL 62794-9265

Complete catalog available at ccthomas.com • books@ccthomas.com

Books sent on approval • Shipping charges: $7.50 min. U.S. / Outside U.S., actual shipping fees will be charged • Prices subject to change without notice

*Savings include all titles shown here and on our web site. For a limited time only.